IDEA / WISE

Kitch

Inspiration & Information for the Do-It-Yourselfer

Jerri Farris

CREATIVE
PUBLISHING
international

CHANHASSEN, MINNESOTA

www.creativepub.com

Copyright © 2004
Creative Publishing international, Inc.
18705 Lake Drive East
Chanhassen, Minnesota 55317
1-800-328-3895
www.creativepub.com

Printed on American Paper by: Quebecor World

10 9 8 7 6 5 4 3 2 1

President/CEO: Michael Eleftheriou
Vice President/Publisher: Linda Ball
Vice President/Retail Sales & Marketing: Kevin Haas

Executive Editor: Bryan Trandem
Creative Director: Tim Himsel
Managing Editor: Michelle Skudlarek
Editorial Director: Jerri Farris

Author: Jerri Farris
Copy Editor: Linnéa Christensen
Art Director: Brad Springer
Mac Designer: Jon Simpson
Technical Illustrator: Earl Slack
Project Manager: Tracy Stanley
Photo Researcher: Julie Caruso
Director of Production Services: Kim Gerber
Production Manager: Stasia Dorn

IdeaWise Kitchens

Library of Congress Cataloging-in-Publication Data

Farris, Jerri.
  Kitchens : inspiration & information for the do-it-yourselfer / Jerri
Farris.
     p. cm. -- (Ideawise)
  ISBN 1-58923-158-9 (sc)
  1. Kitchens--Remodeling--Amateurs' manuals. I. Title. II. Series.
  TH4816.3.K58F37 2004
  643'.3--dc22
                                            2004004622

Table of Contents

Introduction

So, you're dreaming of a dream kitchen. You're not alone, you know. Slightly more than one in four homeowners have the same kind of dream.

It's not surprising. Today's kitchens serve more roles than ever before: cooking area, dining space, home office, entertainment center. Newer homes are built to fit modern lifestyles, but more than half of the houses in America are 30 years old or older; many older kitchens simply don't measure up. Yours may be one of them. Or maybe you have a newer kitchen that just doesn't meet your needs.

It doesn't really matter why you want a new kitchen. *IdeaWise Kitchens* can help point you in the right direction. We'll take you on a tour of more than a hundred kitchens, pointing out ideas and details that may not have occurred to you. Along the way, we're going to define a few industry terms, describe ways you can get the most for your money, give you insider tips from certified kitchen designers, and suggest specific, doable project ideas.

Cooking and sharing food has long been central to family life, a ritual that has traditionally made the kitchen the most important room in the house. The turn of the century brought us life-at-the-speed-of-light, but no matter how tech-savvy we become, nothing can replace the welcoming embrace of a fragrant kitchen or the restorative power of an hour around a table together.

Yes, meals are and will always be important, but cooking itself has become optional. "Home meal replacements" are the biggest things in the grocery industry, and "to-go" is the byword of hundreds of reasonably-priced restaurants. Kitchens remain the foundation of family life, because whether we cook a lot or not, the kitchen is where we live, where we gather, where most of us start and end our days.

Kitchens dominate our homes and therefore the remodeling landscape: There's money in them. Estimates vary by region, but a minor kitchen remodeling project returns somewhere between 78 and 98 percent of its cost in added home value, and a major remodel returns between 72 and 121 percent on resale. That's right. You and your family get to enjoy the new kitchen, and if you sell the house, you get most or all of your money back. The lucky ones among us may even turn a profit. Now, that's a win/win situation.

Careful planning
helped transform this
dowdy kitchen into a
dream come true (see
below right).

Remodeling your kitchen is a big investment in every way—time, money, and energy. Veterans of the process say it's sometimes stressful and challenging. Most also say the results are worth the effort. We can help you make the process less challenging, and here's the secret: Plan…plan…plan.

Long before saws start to whine and dust starts to fly, make a scrapbook of articles and notes on kitchens and kitchen features that interest you and photographs of kitchens you like.

Next, gather the whole family for a discussion of the project. Talk about who uses your current kitchen and how, and discuss the conveniences you'd like to have in the new version. Look through the scrapbook and work together to create a description of your collective dream kitchen. Finally, decide on a budget for the project.

If you're using a contractor or kitchen designer for your project, your scrapbook, description, and budget will be invaluable as you work together. Be sure to bring them to your meetings.

Before you finalize any plans, spend some time considering your needs and wants. Evaluate how and when you cook, where you serve meals and to whom, how often you entertain. Inventory your dishes, silverware, serving pieces, cookware, and linens, and make sure there will be places for all of it. Understanding how you use your kitchen will help you invest your remodeling dollars wisely.

Oh, one more thing: No matter how much time you budget for a remodeling project, it usually takes longer than you think. Your family needs to eat in the meantime. Before you get started, make arrangements to store, heat, and clean up enough to keep body and soul together until the kitchen's back on-line. If you're undertaking a major remodel, having the basics available somewhere else in the house—at least a bar refrigerator, a microwave, and a utility sink—just might save your sanity.

How to Use This Book

The pages of *IdeaWise Kitchens* are packed with images of interesting, attractive, efficient kitchens. And although we hope you enjoy looking at them, they're more than pretty pictures: they're inspiration accompanied by descriptions, facts, and details meant to help you plan your kitchen project wisely.

Some of the kitchens you see here will suit your sense of style, while others may not appeal to you at all. If you're serious about remodeling or building a kitchen, read every page—there's as much to learn in what you don't like as in what you do. Look at each photograph carefully and take notes. The details you gather are the seeds from which ideas for your new kitchen will sprout.

IdeaWise Kitchens contains six chapters: Walls, Floors and Ceilings, Storage and Display, Food Preparation and Cleanup, Dining and Hospitality, Lighting, and Communication and Convenience. In each chapter, you'll find several features, each of which contains a specific type of wisdom.

DesignWise features hints and tips—insider tricks—from professional kitchen planners. Special thanks to DeWitt Talmadge Beall, James Dase, Connie Gustafson, Max Isley, Lori Jo Krengel, and Stephanie Witt.

DollarWise describes money-saving ideas that can be adapted to your own plans and circumstances.

IdeaWise illustrates a clever do-it-yourself project for each topic.

Some chapters also include ***Words to the Wise,*** a glossary of terms that may not be familiar to you.

Another important feature of *IdeaWise Kitchens* is the Resource Guide on pages 130 to 139. The Resource Guide contains as much information as possible about most of the photographs in the book, including contact information for designers and manufacturers when available.

DesignWise

Lori Jo Krengel,
CKD, CBD

Krengel Kitchens
St. Paul, MN

• Build in storage underneath an island. This storage can also act as the countertop support.

• Use the toekick space below your cabinetry. Plan for a pull-out step stool for access to higher cabinets.

• Build around an obstruction and use the space for spices and small item storage.

• If you've fallen in love with see-through bins but can't afford to waste the space on the merely ornamental, don't worry. Place dividers 3" back in the bin, and you can use the space behind the display items.

• Booths and banquettes often include storage space under the seats, but it's often not as easily accessible as other storage areas. Reserve this space for seasonal items and specialty equipment that you need only occasionally.

DollarWise

If you want the look of natural stone but can't afford to do the entire floor, mix a stone tile with a similar-looking ceramic tile or use stone tiles as an accent for a ceramic tile floor.

IdeaWise

According to DeWitt Talmadge Beall, of DeWitt Designer Kitchens, a skylight is the best thing you can do for a ceiling. But what if your kitchen has a second story above it?

No problem: Create a faux skylight. Box out an inverted well, install lighting, and cover the well with sandblasted or obscured glass.

Words to the Wise

What's the difference between *framed* and *frameless* cabinets?

• On **framed cabinets**, the exposed edges of the boxes are covered with flat (face) frames. The doors may be set into the frames or overlay them; the hinges are attached to the frames and the doors.

• On **frameless cabinets**, the exposed edges of the box are covered with edge banding and the doors cover nearly the entire case. The door hinges are attached to the doors and the sides or ends of the boxes.

Which is better?

That's a matter of personal preference. Compare costs on individual styles carefully. Framed cabinets require more materials but often are less exacting to build than frameless. Conversely, frameless cabinets require less material but can be time consuming to build. The structure of frameless cabinets allows for wider doors and better accessibility, but the traditional appearance of framed cabinets is preferable in historic or traditional-style homes. As you shop, remember that door and hardware styles will be dictated to some degree by the frame style you select.

CHAPTER 1

Walls, Floors and Ceilings

Ask most people about remodeling their kitchen, and they'll start talking about new appliances they'd like to have or maybe the new cabinets and countertops they dream of. Those are, after all, the most obvious parts of a kitchen remodeling project. But before the appliances, before the cabinets—before anything else—you need walls, floors, and ceilings.

At first, walls, floors, and ceilings may not sound terribly exciting, but think again. As the largest surfaces in the room, they set the stage for everything else, and they have a major impact on the way your kitchen functions as well as the way it looks.

Right now you may be saying, "Walls? Floors? How could they affect the way a kitchen works?" Easy. Wall space supports cabinets, so more wall space makes more cabinets possible. In the right circumstances, a pass-through streamlines serving and cleaning up. Warmed or cushioned floors make standing more comfortable. Easy-care floors simplify maintenance. Each element is an important part of the whole.

In new construction or major remodeling projects, decisions about walls, floors, and ceilings have to be made long before cabinets are chosen, plumbing is roughed in, or electrical and lighting plans are developed. You can wait to pick most final finishes, but structural decisions, such as choosing subfloor materials, planning additional support for some types of flooring, and deciding whether or not to have soffits, have to be made early in the process.

The number of possibilities for floor and wall coverings can absolutely make your head spin. This chapter will introduce you to some of those possibilities and give you ideas that can guide your selection processes.

Walls

Walls might seem mundane—after all, most kitchens are constructed with simple drywall covered with paint or wallcovering. But after some thought, you'll find that there are more interesting options, including some that give rooms a more architectural quality. The more architectural finishes—brick, wood paneling, and so on—have to be selected before the cabinets and trim.

These homeowners are lucky to have a kitchen with such great natural structure, right?

Wrong. Richness and texture were layered on in a remodeling project, the result of good design, not luck.

You certainly can't tell at first glance, but this kitchen is on the first story of a two-story home. Not exactly conducive to skylights. No problem. Good design to the rescue: A faux skylight floods the room with light.

The home's ordinary drywall walls and ceilings were no barrier to good design either. Cladding walls with real face brick added substance and texture. Installing reclaimed barn wood beams injected aged textures and colors. Speaking of colors, the bricks were painted white to brighten the other earth tones of the room, but in another color scheme, they could easily have been left natural.

Special panels match the dishwasher to the cabinet doors.

Gray grout accents the terra cotta tile, reflecting two tones from the granite countertops.

A pattern repeated from the range adds punch to the border.

The backsplash is the most significant part of a kitchen wall. This is the place to play with color, texture, and light.

Fossils captured in natural stone highlight the spare design of this kitchen. When you incorporate amazing materials like this, don't make them compete for attention with loads of other details. Light them well and let them shine.

Ceramic tile and kitchens go together like peanut butter and jelly. Impervious to water and stains, durable, and reasonably priced—tile backsplashes are attractive, easy to maintain, and affordable. This backsplash mixes textures and colors in border, background, and accent tile to make a strong but subtle statement.

Make the backsplash the focal point of the cooking center by adding a tile medallion or mural. Tile manufacturers offer such features, but it's easy to create one by arranging trim and other specialty tiles in a custom design. Draw full-size plans on brown paper and tape your favorite in place for a day or two before committing. You may surprise yourself with your creativity.

Stainless steel makes an ideal backsplash behind a cooktop. It's watertight, heat resistant, easy to clean, and incredibly durable. In this kitchen, brushed stainless steel protects the walls behind the range and provides a softly reflective surface that contrasts nicely with the concrete countertops. Stainless steel receptacle plates complete the wall's tailored appearance.

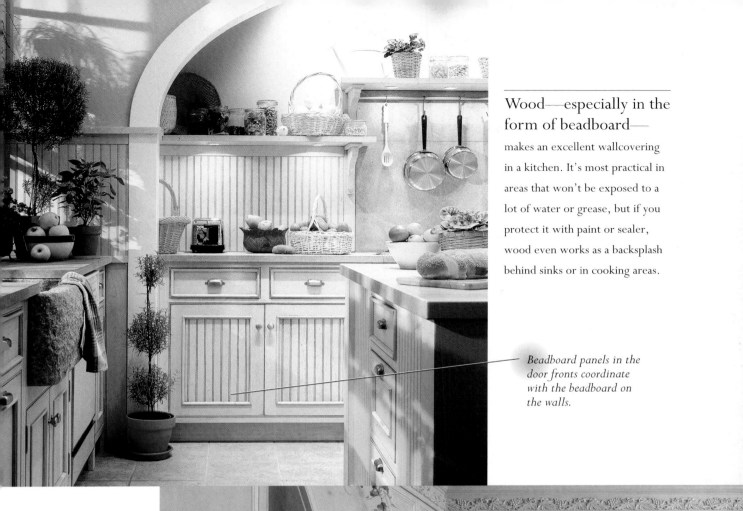

Wood—especially in the form of beadboard—makes an excellent wallcovering in a kitchen. It's most practical in areas that won't be exposed to a lot of water or grease, but if you protect it with paint or sealer, wood even works as a backsplash behind sinks or in cooking areas.

Beadboard panels in the door fronts coordinate with the beadboard on the walls.

Solid-surface material is available in ¼"-thick sheets for use as wall panels and backsplashes. In this kitchen, the green backsplash is detailed with a white stripe to coordinate it with the banded countertops.

Strong color generates interest.

Cherry red demands attention, warming the white subway-style ceramic tile walls. By mixing white tile and painted cabinets with deep color and stainless accents, the homeowners created the illusion of depth within a relatively small space.

Cladding the cooking
center walls with real
face brick warmed and mel-
lowed this brand new kitchen,
adding to its Old World feel.

Soaring ceilings can leave rooms feeling ungrounded, or worse yet, vacant.
Not in this kitchen! By painting the upper walls and window trim white and concentrating vivid
color in the backsplashes, cabinets, countertops, and accessories, these homeowners carved out
warm, cozy space within a large area.

Floors

Glance around a kitchen. What do you see first? Chances are, your brain takes in the cabinets, the counters and backsplash, and then. . .the floor. That's right. The floor. It's typically the largest horizontal surface in the room and undeniably the most used. It's important to choose flooring that fits your taste, lifestyle, and budget.

Bamboo floors work wonderfully in kitchens. Flat grains and natural colors like this are particularly well suited to contemporary kitchens.

The kitchen is a natural dividing line for changing from one floor covering to another. Make sure there's enough contrast that the difference looks intentional. Too close and they could look like a jacket and pants that aren't the same, but also not different enough to go together.

Tile is a durable flooring that lets you achieve a unique, customized look without spending a fortune. In this traditional kitchen, homeowners combined large and small, white and black tiles to create an interesting but subtle background.

Borders give this floor zip.

Flooring Options

Each type of flooring has unique characteristics and installation techniques. Appearance is important, but so are durability, ease-of-care, installation requirements, and environmental impact.

Hardwood

Hardwood floors look and feel warm, are durable, and are easy to clean. True, they can be scratched or dented and need periodic refinishing, but they don't develop wear patterns and can last a lifetime or two. Installation techniques vary.

Tongue-and-groove strip flooring is installed using a power nailer.

Parquet and end grain floors are set in adhesive.

Floating floors are fastened at the tongue-and-groove connections only.

Laminates

Laminate flooring consists of thin layers of plastic laminate bonded to a fiberboard core. It resists scratches and heavy traffic, and is easy to clean. If you're going to install it yourself, remember that it requires a perfectly smooth subfloor.

Laminate flooring is installed like a floating hardwood floor.

Bamboo

Bamboo flooring is durable, attractive, and environmentally sound. Bamboo is actually a grass, and although harvested every three to five years, it continues to regenerate.

Bamboo is installed using the techniques for tongue-and-groove hardwood flooring.

Cork

Cork is comfortable to walk on, easy to clean, and environmentally friendly. The bark of a cork oak tree naturally splits every 9 to 15 years and can be harvested many times without harming the tree.

Cork planks are installed like tongue-and-groove hardwood.

Cork tile is installed with adhesive, similar to parquet flooring.

Vinyl

Inexpensive, easy to clean, and durable, vinyl flooring is available in a huge variety of colors, patterns, and styles.

Sheet vinyl with felt backing is glued to the subfloor.

Sheet vinyl with PVC backing is glued only along the edges, called perimeter-bond.

Vinyl tiles typically come in 12 or 16" squares and are available with or without self-adhesive backing.

Ceramic Tile

The basic categories are:

Glazed ceramic tile: coated with glaze after it's baked, then fired again to produce a hard surface.

Porcelain tile: extremely dense and hard, and naturally water resistant. Its color runs throughout its thickness.

Quarry tile: unglazed, porous tile that's softer and thicker than glazed tile. It needs to be sealed periodically.

All ceramic tile flooring is installed with the same basic process: set the tile in thin-set mortar, then grout it. It's very doable, but requires time for planning and for the step-by-step process.

Natural Stone Tile

Granite, marble, and slate tiles are the most common stone products for floors. Granite and marble are generally sold with polished or sealed surfaces. Slate tiles, formed by cleaving the stone along natural faults, have textured surfaces.

Natural stone is installed like ceramic tile. The materials and installation are quite expensive. You may be able to find discounts on the stone, but don't skimp when it comes to installation materials.

Resilient flooring typically is the least expensive kitchen flooring material, as well as the simplest and quickest to install. If the price, easy installation, and simple maintenance appeal to you, but not the traditional patterns, look again. Today's sheet vinyl introduces the look of more costly floor coverings at more reasonable prices.

Plank-flooring-patterned sheet vinyl graces the floor of this fabulous farm-style kitchen.

The resilient flooring in this elegant kitchen mimics the look of ceramic tile.

Accent squares in the flooring coordinate with the counters and backsplash.

The warmth, beauty, and availability of hardwood flooring make it very popular in North American kitchens, especially in the East and Midwest. Solid wood flooring is relatively expensive, but with the right finishes, it's durable and needs only frequent vacuuming and occasional damp mopping to look its best. Although wood can be scratched and dented, it also can be returned to its original glory with periodic refinishing, a factor that makes it cost effective over time.

Plank hardwood flooring complements the rustic look of this kitchen. The color variations of the planks go well with the unusual drawer fronts.

Strip hardwood floors blend well in many styles of kitchens. The warm tones of this hardwood floor provide a lovely background for this Euro-style kitchen.

Laminate flooring is available in many colors and textures. You can choose from patterns designed to replicate the look of materials as diverse as hardwood, ceramic tile, and even concrete.

Laminate flooring resists scratches and heavy wear from traffic, and it's easy to maintain with light cleaning. Wood patterns are common, but not the only options.

Cork—either vinyl-coated or waxed—is resilient, impervious to water and insects, and easy on the knees and feet. In this kitchen, cork flooring in a checkerboard pattern repeats the natural-and-black combination used throughout the room.

*Design*Wise

DeWitt Talmadge Beall

DeWitt Designer Kitchens
Studio City, CA

Simplicity gives a design power. Try these ideas:

Floors

• Choose a floor covering that reflects the color of the cabinets or the counters/backsplash.

• Consider installing radiant heating mats under stone or tile. They make a hard floor more friendly and are an efficient source of heat.

• Continuous floors are good, but be careful with natural hardwood running into laundry areas. Prevent water damage by installing a sheet metal washer tray that includes its own drain.

Walls

• Take a stone or tile backsplash to the ceiling behind a range or cooktop and float a hood against it.

• Clad sections of the wall in panels to match the cabinetry, and float shelves or rail systems against it.

Ceilings

• Skylights are the best thing you can do for a ceiling. Choose units that can be opened and closed with remote controls, feature Low-E glass, and have several modes of light control.

• Uplight the ceiling with dimmable xenon lights placed on the tops of wall cabinets set approximately 15" from the ceiling. Position the lights forward behind the crown for maximum dispersion and to eliminate hot spots on the walls.

Ceilings

Compared to other elements in the kitchen, the choices for ceiling surfaces are relatively limited. In most kitchens, the ceilings are constructed with a drywall base and covered with paint or wallcovering. Those are the most common but not the only alternatives, of course. For something different, try plaster, a mural, painted or stained beadboard, wood panels, or decorative beams.

Soaring white ceiling, white walls, white cabinets, white counters, white floors.

So what makes this space feel vibrant rather than like the inside of a refrigerator? Creativity, innovation, and color.

Start with the flying cornice bridge. This unusual structure wraps the room with color, defining the space without closing it off. Although it's sophisticated, the bridge isn't complicated. The ends rest on the cabinets and the center is supported by polished metal rods anchored in the ceiling.

Next, the remarkable backsplash. Made entirely of glass, the etched glass design is lit from below by a neon tube running through a channel.

And don't forget the floor. Framed by a toekick and the transition to the adjacent flooring, color warms this white tile floor.

If you decide to add details to a ceiling, make sure the style, shape, size, and color are well suited to the room.

Creativity, innovation and color.

The rustic beams accenting the ceiling of this southwestern kitchen add a sort of sunbleached authenticity to the room.

The ceiling in this breakfast nook is steeped in tradition. Paneling, coffers, and traditional carvings pay tribute to the homeowners' Scandinavian heritage.

Extra details make ornamental beams look more architectural. Sandwiched between cove molding and another line of trim molding, bearing blocks provide substance to these decorative beams.

Light fixtures recessed into the beams lighten and brighten the room.

*Idea*Wise

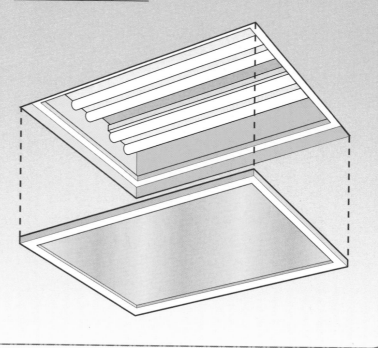

According to DeWitt Talmadge Beall, of DeWitt Designer Kitchens, a skylight is the best thing you can do for a ceiling. But what if your kitchen has a second story above it?

No problem: Create a faux skylight. Box out an inverted well, install lighting, and cover the well with sandblasted or obscured glass.

Layer on the details.

Paneling, beams, and posts

give character to new construction.

Drywall and paint might have been too little. A variety of coverings might have been too much. But like Goldilocks, these homeowners found a solution that was just right. Pine sheathing covers the walls and ceilings, unifying the various angles and planes of the room without camouflaging them.

Look carefully at the points where the walls and ceiling meet: The planks are matched up with the precision of a hand-tailored pinstriped suit. This kind of attention to detail marks the difference between the work of a craftsman and an amateur.

If you decide to do something like this in your own kitchen, plan, plan, plan. Measure, calculate, and make detailed drawings before you make the first cut. The time you invest in planning will pay off in a professional-looking job.

CHAPTER 2

Storage and Display

Let's face it: cabinets make or break a kitchen. They establish how the room looks, and how it works. The style of the room, its color scheme, traffic patterns, level of convenience—they all start with the cabinets. And if you're building or doing a major remodel, one more thing needs to start there: the budget. Cabinets represent the single largest investment in a typical kitchen.

If your current cabinets provide enough storage, but you just don't like the way they look, consider painting or refacing them. Painting in an option only for wood cabinets, but both wood and laminate cabinets can be refaced by installing new cabinet doors, drawer fronts, and matching veneer for covering face frames and cabinet ends. Refacing costs more than painting but much less than installing all new cabinets.

If you decide to go all the way, do it right. Make a budget, evaluate your real needs and wants, and learn as much as you can about cabinet design and construction, especially if you're working on your own. If you're using a kitchen designer or contractor, you can rely on their knowledge and experience, but you still need to be prepared to make wise choices. At the end of the day, you're the one who's going to be living with these decisions—and paying for them.

Start your research right here. This chapter is filled with information, ideas, and photographs of attractive, interesting, efficient kitchens. Take notes and have fun.

Cabinets

The next few pages will introduce you to ready-to-assemble (RTA), stock, semi-custom, and custom cabinetry. Learn as much as you can about each option so you can fairly evaluate quality, price, and durability as well as the available styles and finishes. Once you've decided on a type and style, take advantage of every resource available to you when it comes to designing the cabinet layout. As we've said, you're likely to live with this choice for a long time.

Ready-to-assemble (RTA) cabinets are available through home centers and furnishings retailers. The cases are standard, but you select the style of doors, end panels, and accessories you want to include. You need to measure your kitchen and create a plan, but most stores offer in-store kitchen designers who will review your layout and give you hints and options.

Several retailers offer kitchen planning guides, including downloadable kitchen planning tools, that let you try out various configurations within the dimensions of your kitchen.

Words to the Wise

What's the difference between *framed* and *frameless* cabinets?

• On **framed cabinets,** the exposed edges of the boxes are covered with flat (face) frames. The doors may be set into the frames or overlay them; the hinges are attached to the frames and the doors.

• On **frameless cabinets,** the exposed edges of the box are covered with edge banding and the doors cover nearly the entire case. The door hinges are attached to the doors and the sides or ends of the boxes.

Which is better?

That's a matter of personal preference. Compare costs on individual styles carefully. Framed cabinets require more materials but often are less exacting to build than frameless. Conversely, frameless cabinets require less material but can be time consuming to build. The structure of frameless cabinets allows for wider doors and better accessibility, but the traditional appearance of framed cabinets is preferable in historic or traditional-style homes. As you shop, remember that door and hardware styles will be dictated to some degree by the frame style you select.

Stock cabinets, available through home centers, are offered in a range of standard sizes, usually in 3" increments. A limited variety of door styles and colors can be purchased off the shelf or delivered within a few days. Some specialized accessories or units may have to be special ordered. You can install them yourself, take advantage of the installation services offered through the home center, or hire a carpenter.

Semi-custom cabinets

are manufactured in hundreds of standard sizes, finishes and styles. You can buy these cabinets through home centers, kitchen designers, and contractors.

Following a plan that you or you and a designer have created, your cabinets are built to order according to the manufacturer's standard specifications. You can install the cabinets yourself, use the installation services offered through the home center, hire a carpenter, or have your contractor install them.

Custom cabinets can be built by a custom manufacturer or by a cabinet shop. In either case, you get—and pay for—high-quality materials and workmanship, practically an infinite number of details, accessories, and sizes, and specialized styling. Custom cabinets typically are installed by a contractor or by the cabinetmakers themselves.

Guidelines from the National Kitchen and Bath Association recommend that every kitchen includes at least five storage or organizing items located between 15 and 48" above the finished floor. Cabinets of every kind—from RTA to custom—can be outfitted with accessories to organize and store kitchen utensils. Of course, the price of the cabinets goes up with every built-in convenience. Fortunately, many accessories are available as add-ons, so you can continue to accessorize your cabinets over time.

Before you order new cabinets, investigate accessory options. Retail stores, catalogs, and Internet sites devoted to organization typically offer a wide variety of cabinet accessories. Compare features and prices of built-in accessories to add-ons of similar quality, and create a plan that offers the most convenience possible within your budget.

Remember that add-on accessories have to be installed. That's not an issue if you're doing the work yourself, but if you're hiring someone to do it, be sure to factor the cost of installation into the comparison between built-ins and add-ons.

Spice drawers are handy when you're baking—individual bottles can be identified and selected easily.

These slide-out drawers have heavy-duty runners with special guides for side stability. The plate rack as well as the lid holder are made of solid beech and aluminum. The sturdiness and stability of these drawers make them easy to use and reliable for many years.

Pull-out, expanding shelves bring the contents of the corner out to you.

Revolving corner systems are efficient and affordable.

Roll-out shelves improve the efficiency of nearly every cabinet, from large pantries to narrow tray cabinets. Plan carefully and invest wisely. There are few things more frustrating in a kitchen than flimsy, poorly supported shelves and glides that don't work smoothly.

Try looking at corners from a different angle.

The corner. You know the story—nothing but wasted space, awkward angles, and traffic tie-ups. Forget all that. Handled with care, corners become usable, attractive spaces—sometimes even the highlight of the kitchen.

Upper cabinets telescope down toward the corner,

focusing attention on the elegant windows and the magnificent view from this urban kitchen. A display shelf disguises the potentially awkward gap at the back, and an angled double-bowl sink nestles into the remaining space.

No soaring windows?

No problem—create your own view. Set the sink in an angled cabinet recessed from the profile of the base cabinets, and add lighted display space above. The interesting profile of this arrangement is enhanced by edge banding on the counters, island, and backsplash.

Interior lighting adds impact.

The most useful storage space is between hip and shoulder height, according to ergonomic experts. Dropping a wall cabinet all the way to the counter-top, connecting the wall cabinet to the base, makes a wall cabinet work like a china cabinet. The right trim and finish can make it look like one, too.

Far from a liability, this corner became the foundation of a baking center. The base cabinet adjacent to the corner was recessed and its countertop lowered to create convenient workspace. Narrow cabinets on either side extend all the way to the countertop, framing the space; an appliance garage completes the arrangement. The recessed workspace base leaves room for the folding door and swing-out shelves of the corner unit to operate. A similar arrangement makes the space in the upper corner fully functional. Open display shelves round out the end of the cabinets.

*Design*Wise

Lori Jo Krengel,
CKD, CBD

Krengel Kitchens
St. Paul, MN

• Build in storage underneath an island. This storage can also act as the countertop support.

• Use the toekick space below your cabinetry. Plan for a pull-out step stool for access to higher cabinets.

• Build around an obstruction and use the space for spices and small item storage.

• If you've fallen in love with see-through bins that display pasta, grain, and other items but can't afford to waste the space on the merely ornamental, don't worry. Place dividers 3" back in the bin, and you can use the space behind the display items.

• Booths and banquettes often include storage space under the seats, but it's often not as easily accessible as other storage areas. Reserve this space for seasonal items and specialty equipment that you need only occasionally.

Decked out with dark stain and glass doors,
an angled upper cabinet acts as an accent piece. A lighted interior
focuses attention on the items displayed there.

*Continuing the light
trim molding integrates
the display piece into
the other cabinets.*

Denim-like textures and colors on the beadboard ceiling, backsplash tiles, and hand-painted stools set the stage for the homeowner's collection of classic and contemporary blue and white collectibles. Complementary natural tones temper the blue and warm the white of the doors and drawers of the base cabinets, countertops, and soffits. Together they create a clean, spare look that suits the rest of the house as well as the homeowner's lifestyle.

Anxious to display as many of their treasured pieces as possible, the homeowners crafted this simple but elegant display piece from birch 1 x 6s and stained it to match the ceiling. Look at the shelves closely: ⅛" grooves have been routed into the shelves to support and stabilize the plates on display.

If you can't decide between a window and one more upper cabinet, choose both.

Windows make dramatic backdrops for display cabinets. This cabinet has a glass panel in back and glass doors in front. The crystal and glassware inside reflect and refract sunshine, lighting up the kitchen on sunny days.

*Idea*Wise

Tired of a tripping over shoes in the back hall? Cap the end of a cabinet run with a low, open bench built to match. Top the bench with a cushion, and the clever storage piece becomes a convenient place to change shoes as well.

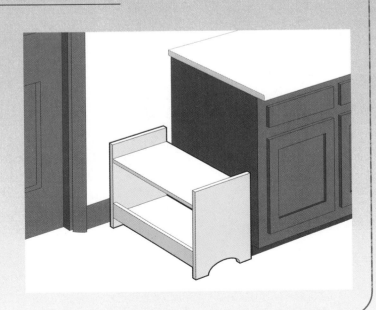

Combining finishes or colors creates an interesting, custom look.

The pine cabinetry in this kitchen is the same throughout, despite the appearance that individual sections are freestanding pieces. To create this impression, the designers used color. The base cabinets and island are one color, the wine bar a lighter version of that color, and the cabinets framing the window are a green that complements the countertops. This simple technique sets separate areas apart and coordinates them with one another without matching.

Color accentuates the positive in this traditional kitchen.

Painted trim molding matches the island and built-in display piece, focusing attention in all the right places. The white countertops on the perimeter cabinets blend into the white tile backsplash, giving the island's rich marble countertop the prominence it deserves.

Hand-painted tiles and cheerful collectibles complete this colorful picture.

Islands provide convenient space for meal preparation and informal dining as well as storage and display space.

This multi-level island is home to a sink, food preparation area, informal eating area, and a wine rack.

The raised countertop provides casual dining space and shields the sink and work spaces from view. One of the disadvantages of an open-plan kitchen is that meal preparation areas can be seen from other spaces—often from a family or great room. That's not a problem if you're a tidy cook, but most families find that there are times when a little camouflage is welcome.

The island's counter and finish match the rest of the cabinets, which keeps it from dominating the room.

A wine rack tucked under the counter supplies storage without using much floor space.

The stained shoe provides a graceful transition between the painted molding and the hardwood floor.

This one-level island provides an uninterrupted work surface as well as casual dining space. The handsomely crafted legs supporting the dining extension give the island the look of fine furniture.

Open shelves cap off the island with display space. Open shelves like this can be used to show off special accessories or to house books, especially cookbooks.

Recessed lights supply the general lighting for this kitchen, but pendants provide attractive task lighting for the island. Controlled separately by a rheostat, the pendants can be turned up while you're cooking and then dimmed for meals.

Make sure the aisles around an island remain at least 42" wide in a one-cook kitchen and at least 48" wide in a multi-cook kitchen.

This island provides most of the food preparation area in this kitchen. A small sink nestled at the end of the island provides a handy source of water for those chores.

Glass panel doors echo the window style.

Open, recessed shelves are great places to store large serving pieces or even cookware, if it's attractive.

A plate rack on the side of the island, just opposite the sink, is an unusual touch—very handy for putting plates away after a meal. The island itself is stained to match the base cabinets, but the bookshelf at the end is finished to match the uppers. Combining finishes is an easy way to get the furniture look that's so popular in today's kitchens.

Bowed cabinets soften the ends of this island. Guidelines developed by the National Kitchen and Bath Association suggest that open counter corners be clipped or cut along a radius to eliminate sharp corners. Rounding the corners of this island made them safer as well as more interesting.

If rounded corners appeal to you, consider this: MDF (medium-density fiberboard) lends itself to curves much more easily than other cabinet materials. When shopping for MDF cabinets, make sure the tops, bottoms, and sides of the cabinet cases are ⅝" or ¾" thick. Thinner materials—typically ¼"—are fine for cabinet backs, which don't support any weight, but the rest of the case needs the strength of more substantial materials.

When properly finished, MDF makes beautiful, durable cabinets, but it's important to note that water completely destroys unfinished MDF. Since many kitchen tasks start and end with water, it's absolutely mandatory that all edges and surfaces of MDF cabinets be completely covered with laminate or paint. The faces of doors and drawers on many high-quality MDF cabinets are finished with a PVC coating and paint, an excellent system.

Countertops

DollarWise

Save more expensive materials for smaller, specialty areas—marble for a baking center or stainless steel surrounding a cooktop—and install less expensive materials in others. As long as the colors and textures are complementary, combinations make kitchens more interesting.

The style and color of its countertops have tremendous impact on a kitchen's appearance, but countertop materials are more than just a pretty (sur)face. Indeed, those materials affect the way you use and clean your kitchen. With some materials, you have be careful not to stain, scratch, or scorch the surface. Others demand specific cleaning routines. Heat-resistant surfaces, such as granite, stainless steel, tile, and other solid surfaces, make it easy to transfer hot pans or dishes from range or oven.

Edge treatments also play an important part in the appearance and function of countertops. Decorative profiles, color banding, and mixed materials all create additional interest.

Generally, it's best to select your cabinets and flooring materials, then choose materials, colors, and textures for your countertops.

The National Kitchen and Bath Association guidelines suggest that every kitchen include at least two work counter heights: one at 28 to 36" above the floor, and one at 36 to 45" above the floor. The guidelines also suggest that kitchens under 150 square feet have 132" of usable counter frontage, and kitchens over 150 square feet have at least 198" of usable counter frontage. (Complete guidelines are available from the National Kitchen and Bath Association—see page 140 for further information.)

Natural stone offers a cool surface, excellent for handling dough, especially pastry.

This California contemporary-style kitchen features maple cabinets topped with maple countertops. Granite counters surround the range and extend from the island, providing excellent surfaces for food preparation and casual dining. Paired with the mellow maple of the upper counter and the aged, distressed green finish of the island, the green-gold jupurana granite is particularly appealing.

Butcher-block countertops can be scratched and can absorb stains and odors. They're resistant to heat but will burn if exposed to enough heat. You can sand and reseal the surface to repair scratches and minor damage.

To prevent warping, seal both sides of butcher-block countertops with nontoxic polyurethane. Cutting board areas, well away from water sources, can be left unsealed; just rub them periodically with mineral, tung, or linseed oil. Don't use vegetable oil, which turns rancid over time.

Granite counters have smooth, cool, heat-resistant surfaces that also resist marks and scratches, though they do absorb some oils and stains. Important point: Damaged granite counters can't be repaired—replacement is the only option.

Portuguese tile gives this countertop distinction, but the definitive touch of style comes in the edge treatment for the undermount sinks. Switching from the white tile to blue trim defines the sink areas and helps coordinate the front edge treatment with the rest of the counter as well as with the homeowner's collection of blue-and-white collectibles.

Tile is impervious to water and stains, and highly resistant to scratches. In fact, the grout is the only part of a tile countertop that's susceptible to damage from everyday wear and tear. Using epoxy grout reduces staining, mildew, and other damage on countertops and backsplashes.

This kitchen takes advantage of two fine countertop materials. The cabinets are topped with white solid-surface countertops; the island cooking area boasts black granite. This kitchen might have been bland with all white countertops or too heavy with all black. Mixing materials produced a combination of strengths and a nicely balanced look.

Granite makes excellent counters, especially for an island like this: It resists heat, marks, and scratches. Granite counters do require some care in use, though. They can absorb oils and odors, and can be damaged if subjected to enough force. Major damage is an expensive proposition because granite can't be repaired, only replaced.

Concrete countertops blend seamlessly into the decor of this sleek, spare kitchen. Smooth, heat and stain resistant, and easy to clean up, the warm, aged finish and natural look of concrete is suitable to a broad range of kitchen designs.

Pre-cast concrete countertops generally are shipped to the job site and cut to fit with a diamond blade on a skill saw, wet or dry. They also can be cast in place.

Either way, they need to be sealed with a lacquer sealer. Fabricators recommend paste waxing concrete countertops every three months and resealing them every year or two.

Most manufacturers recommend mild, non-abrasive, non-ammoniated soap for daily cleaning. Avoid abrasive soaps, pads, and cleansers.

Concrete counters are prone to cracking, but the typical hairline cracks don't affect their structural integrity. Although they can be patched, many people consider cracks part of the look of concrete counters. Stains can be removed by sanding with 100-grit sandpaper and then reapplying sealer and wax.

Stainless steel counters and backsplashes work with stainless steel appliances

to make this galley kitchen as easy to look at as it is to clean. The stainless surfaces softly reflect light, making the space seem more spacious than it actually is.

When it comes to resistance to heat, water, and damage, stainless steel is the absolute champion. It lasts practically forever and, as you see here, can be formed into edging, backsplashes, and sinks. (Welding a prefabricated stainless sink into a countertop is a less expensive option than an integral sink, however.)

For sturdy countertops, use 14 or 16 gauge steel (the smaller the number, the thicker the steel) over ¾" plywood—the plywood adds strength and muffles sound. For backsplashes, 18 to 22 gauge, steel is fine.

Use mild detergent, baking soda, or vinegar diluted in water to clean stainless steel. If you are using any kind of an abrasive, clean in the direction of the grain. Never use bleach, and avoid steel wool—fine particles left in the surface will eventually rust, making it look like the stainless itself is rusting. Scratches can't be repaired, but that's not a problem—most people like the satin look they produce.

Marble tops this island baking center, just waiting for pastry to be rolled or cookies to be cut on its smooth, cool surface. Marble scratches somewhat easily, and, like granite, it isn't repairable. It's impervious to heat but absorbs oils and some odors. Because it's rather porous, it can be stained, especially by acidic foods. Seal it with a penetrating sealer every few years.

There are ways to make natural stone countertops more affordable. Research suppliers carefully—prices vary widely, depending on where the stone is quarried and dressed and how it's finished. If you need only a small piece for an island, you might find a bargain at a local stone yard. If seams are necessary, talk with your designer or contractor about how they'll be handled.

Solid-surface countertops are easy to restore. Light sanding will remove surface scratches, burns, and stains; more significant damage requires professional restoration. Since its introduction in the early 1970s, solid surface materials have quickly become one of the most popular counter materials on the market. They resist heat, marks, and scratches. And because the color goes all the way through the material, minor damage simply can be sanded or polished away.

Solid-surface materials easily can be cut and shaped, so interesting contours, elaborate edge profiles, and integral drainboards are possible. And again, because the material is solid, these counters can be used with undermount sinks.

Thinner solid-surface material is available for backsplashes, such as the one shown here.

Plastic laminate—available in a truly vast variety—can be found to complement virtually any decorating scheme. It works well in cooking centers like this because it doesn't absorb stains, oils, or odors. For decades, plastic laminate has been the countertop of choice in millions of homes because it's inexpensive, durable, and easy to maintain. Although the laminate itself is quite water resistant, the substrate beneath is not, so seams and sink cutouts have to be sealed thoroughly.

You have to be careful with plastic laminate countertops—they can be scratched, chipped, or scorched. But if the worst happens, it's the easiest and least expensive type of countertop material to replace.

Light gray, granite-look laminate counters blend well with these traditional white cabinets. Solid-core laminate has color all the way through the body, which eliminates the dark line that can be seen on a self edge of a light colored piece of standard laminate.

Solid-core laminate may not be for everyone—it's more expensive and not available in as many colors and patterns. If you plan to use standard laminate, consider bevel-edge molding or wood or metal nosing to cover the dark line of the kraft-paper core.

CHAPTER *3*

Food Preparation and *Cleanup*

According to Craig Claiborne, "For those who love it, cooking is at once child's play and adult joy."

Even for those who love to cook—maybe especially for them—it's more fun to work in a kitchen where high-quality appliances, workspaces, and storage areas are thoughtfully arranged. Successful kitchens start with careful observation of the people who cook there—who they are and how they like to work. For example, how many people typically work in the kitchen at once? Are they right- or left-handed? Average height, taller than average, or shorter than average? What physical limitations do they have? It's only when you've answered questions like these that you're ready to begin planning the food preparation and clean-up areas of a kitchen.

If you're replacing appliances, there are other important questions to ask yourself. After all, in a typical kitchen, the investment in appliances is second only to cabinets. Start by considering how your family cooks, day to day. If most of your cooking is really just warming prepared food, sophisticated appliances may not be worth the money. On the other hand, if you don't feel you've cooked unless you've dirtied every pot and pan in the house, appliances with all the latest bells and whistles may be good investments. Only you can determine what you truly need and how much of what you want fits within your budget.

When it comes to kitchen remodeling, space needs to be budgeted as carefully as money. Large appliances and wall oven/cooktop combinations take floor and counter space that could be used in other ways—preparation areas or storage space, for example. In smaller kitchens, there are simply fewer square feet available, which means you'll need to conserve wherever possible.

Throughout this chapter, you'll find ideas and suggestions about how to create an efficient, comfortable, enjoyable kitchen.

Meal Preparation

The three basic centers of operation in any kitchen are food prep, cooking, and cleanup. The food prep areas involve the refrigerator and sink; cooking—the cooktop, oven, and microwave; cleanup—the sink, dishwasher, and recycling areas. Ideally, these centers of operations should be placed in convenient relationships to one another. The standard work triangle is a practical starting point and often leads to well-designed kitchens, but it's by no means the only way to approach the issue.

Dual sinks certainly aren't a necessity, but in multi-cook kitchens, they're practical luxuries. In this kitchen, a large two-bowl sink for food preparation and cleanup sits in the corner by the window, and a smaller food prep sink rests in the island. The deep bowl and the pull-out sprayer faucet on the food prep sink make it a handy place to clean vegetables, rinse dishes, or fill pots.

This large kitchen has another luxury—lots of counter space. Every kitchen should have a food preparation area near the sink, at least 36" of uninterrupted counter to the left of the sink for right-handed people or to the right for left-handed people. Multi-cook kitchens should include 36" of counter space for each cook.

The double wall ovens here are positioned so one or the other is at a convenient height for almost anyone. The top oven is in a convenient position for a cook of average height, but the lower one can be reached by smaller or seated persons. Plus, the ovens are adjacent to a long expanse of solid-surface countertop, perfect landing space for dishes straight out of the oven.

If you're planning to have a window like this, remember that you'll want to open it! This double-hung is within reach, but that's not always the case. If there's too much distance between you and the window, a double-hung is awkward. Casement windows, which crank open, are easy to operate as long as the handle is within reach.

With a bar stool of just the right height, a cook can comfortably sit while working— the island's height and the countertop's overhang are designed for that.

Side-by-side refrigerators, which often include through-the-door ice / water dispensers, require less clearance for the swing of the doors than other configurations.

This sink and refrigerator are aligned with one another, with work-space between. This arrangement makes it easy to prepare and serve meals and snacks. With a minimum of steps, you can pull out milk for breakfast, wash and cut fruit for a snack, or cook a multi-course meal. With the island so well positioned in relationship to the sink and re-frigerator, even cleaning up after a meal is a breeze.

When shopping for a refrigerator, take a tape measure along. Evaluate the interior space and lay-out as well as the door swing clearance. Don't forget to check the noise level—no one wants to listen to the refrigerator hum all evening.

The built-in refrigerator is disguised with cabinetry panel fronts to create a custom look. Built-in refrigerators are popular, but quite expensive. If a built-in refrigerator suits your taste but not your budget, check out the alternatives. Several manufacturers offer models with designer doors that give you a built-in look. They may not have quite the same custom fit, but they don't take as big a bite out of your appliance budget either.

In an interesting twist, this kitchen includes a sink in one island, a cooktop in another, and a refrigerator on a diagonal from each. Counter space located to one side of the refrigerator is especially convenient when it comes time to put away the groceries. The raised countertops surrounding each island provide good landing space and screen the work areas from view.

Bottom-freezer and top-freezer refrigerators typically are less expensive than side-by-side models. They cost less over time, too, since they're more energy efficient.

*Design*Wise

James R. Dase, CKD, CBD

Abruzzo Kitchens
Schaumburg, IL

• The right sink improves the flow of work. Sinks with one extra-large basin and one smaller basin give you an area for cleaning or soaking large items and another to use in the meantime. Installing the garbage disposal in the larger basin gives you a larger space to clean heavily soiled items. A basin rack on the floor of the sink protects the surface from scratches and dents.

• Faucets with pull-out spray heads are great for easy sink cleanups and for filling large stockpots on the counter.

• To make cleanup easier, position a pull-out waste receptacle below the chopping area. If you compost organic materials, choose a small, easy-to-clean receptacle. Make sure the kitchen includes at least two pull-out waste receptacles, one for trash and one for recycling.

• Keep frequently used spices near the cooktop, in racks on a nearby wall cabinet door, or in a drawer with special inserts. To retain freshness, keep spice refills away from the heat of the cooking center.

Clean-up Center

The major elements of a clean-up center are the sink, dishwasher, and garbage/recycling area. Like the folk wisdom about real estate, when it comes to the clean-up center, the three most important factors are: location, location, and location.

Despite advances in dishwasher technology, doing the dishes still starts at the sink. To simplify the transfer of dishes and utensils, place the dishwasher within 36" of the main sink. Allow 21" of standing room on one side or the other—both if you can. If doing the dishes is a group effort at your house, make sure more than one person can reach the dishwasher at a time.

The quality of a stainless steel sink is measured by the thickness of the steel, the amount of chromium and nickel it contains, and the effectiveness of the sound control.

With the dishwasher next to the sink, there's plenty of room on both sides for the clean-up crew. Look through the glass cabinet doors—you can see that even the arrangement of the dishes has been well planned.

By putting special, hand-wash-only glasses above the sink and the more commonly used, dishwasher-safe dishes and glasses to the side of the dishwasher, the homeowner created an efficient traffic pattern for putting away the dishes.

This dishwasher is positioned to eliminate bending. If you or a family member has difficulty bending down, raise the dishwasher 9 to 12" off the floor. It will be easier to load and unload the dishes, and you'll have a raised counter, which adds an interesting design element and may be more comfortable for some users.

Undermount sinks don't have edges to collect grime or allow water to seep into cabinets like self-rimmed sinks. If you want an undermount sink, you'll need tile, solid-surface, or stone countertops.

Each of these slide-out drawers conceals two trash cans behind a matching drawer front. Drawers of this sort have to support a fair amount of weight, so sturdy, high-quality glides and frames are a must.

When it comes to garbage/recycling areas, size matters. You need enough space for containers capable of holding several days' worth of trash and recycling. As any parent—especially parents of teenagers—will tell you, it's irritating to have food wrappers fall out on your feet when you open the door to the trash area. So, create space for large bins and a place to store trash bags and other supplies. If everything's within reach, maybe someone else will take out the trash for a change.

The sink is the most frequently used piece of equipment in a kitchen, and its size and placement are important. A standard sink is 6 to 8" deep, but the trend now is toward 10- to 12"-deep models. Combined with high-neck faucets, deep sinks are great for handling big pots and lots of dishes, and they make it easier to keep the water in the sink rather than all over the counters and the floors.

Deep sinks are not always the best choice, though. Taller people may find it uncomfortable to bend over a deep sink; raising the countertop a few inches may make it easier and more comfortable for them. On the other hand, shorter or seated users appreciate lower countertops and shallower sinks. Plan ahead for this—minor adaptations make a major difference.

A colored solid-surface countertop can be joined to a more traditional white sink, as in this Arts and Crafts kitchen. There are no seams or ridges either. The man-made composites of solid-surface materials can be fabricated in an almost infinite variety of shapes and sizes. Computerized cutting systems allow fabricators to create intricate, custom sink designs with ease.

Solid-surface sinks are second only to stainless steel when it comes to consumer choices for upscale kitchens. Why? Simple—they're quiet, easy to clean, and stain- and scratch-resistant. Any stains or scratches that do occur can be buffed or sanded out.

Installing a solid surface sink isn't a do-it-yourself project—they have to be fabricated and installed by trained and licensed craftspeople.

With this unique storage feature, these homeowners accomplished two important tasks: adding display storage and opening the room to the stairs. A project like this takes nothing but a few boards, a little trim, and a free afternoon.

Stainless steel sinks are always appropriate, especially combined with stainless appliances. Even with the number of shapes now available, traditional sinks like this one—rectangular with rounded corners—remain the most popular. Experts say rectangular sinks hold more, and rounded corners are easier to clean than square ones.

When it comes to economy and serviceability, you can't beat self-rimmed, stainless steel sinks. Typically, the least expensive and easiest to install of all sink styles, they never seem to go out of style. To ensure durability, 20 gauge steel is good, 18 is better—remember, the lower the number, the thicker the steel. The best sinks contain 18 percent chromium and have an undercoating on the bottom and sides of the basins to make them less noisy.

Stainless steel sinks are available with either satin or mirror finishes. Satin finishes are easy to maintain because minor scratches can be buffed out with a scouring pad. Mirror finishes scratch easily, so save them for sinks that are used gently, such as in a bar or butler's pantry.

Undivided, apron-front, farm-style sinks are everywhere these days, especially in model homes and design magazines. People who cook or entertain a lot like them because they can hold several large pots and pans with room to spare. These sinks are great for the right type of cook, but they're also quite expensive. Make sure it truly fits your cooking and living style before you invest in any sink—if you're like most people, you'll use it more than any other fixture in your kitchen.

Words to the Wise

Kitchen sinks can be categorized according to how they are mounted in the countertop.

• **Self-rimmed sinks** have rolled edges that rest directly on the countertop. This is the most common style because it's the easiest to install and typically the least expensive. The drawback is that the joint between the sink and countertop attracts dirt and has to be cleaned regularly.

• **Flush-mounted sinks** are recessed into the counter to sit flush with the surface. They blend nicely with countertops and are easy to keep clean.

• **Undermount sinks** fit below the countertop. They're often used with solid-surface, tile, or stone countertops, They can't be used with laminate countertops because the edges aren't waterproof from the top and from the sides.

• **Integral sinks** are molded basins that are actually part of the countertops. Stainless steel and solid-surface countertops often include integral sinks, which are attractive, virtually seamless, and very expensive. Minor damage can usually be buffed out of these materials, but major damage means the whole unit has to be replaced, an expensive proposition.

Enameled cast-iron sinks are attractive, extremely durable, and economical. A near automatic choice at one time, current trends have diminished their popularity. They're still excellent sinks, however.

Although others are available, self-rimming styles are common. Many homeowners searching for reasonably priced sinks find themselves considering both enameled cast-iron and stainless steel. Enamel sinks are available in many colors and shapes, which is a factor for many people. On the other hand, good quality models typically are more expensive than stainless steel, and the thickness of the material leaves the interior of an enamel sink slightly smaller than a stainless sink with the same dimensions. In some styles, the weight of the cast-iron may require special supports.

Today's enamel sinks don't chip easily, but they do have limits, and dropping heavy items in them may cause damage. Small chips can be repaired with a material sold at many hardware stores and home centers, but the repaired area will never look exactly the same.

Stain-resistant surfaces make routine maintenance simple; avoid abrasive cleaners.

Although self-rimmed styles are more typical, enameled cast-iron sinks are available in trendy styles and colors like this red, apron-front model.

*Idea*Wise

If you like islands but your kitchen doesn't have room for a permanent version, make one you can use when preparing meals and tuck back against a wall when it's not needed.

Start with a vintage table. Use a jigsaw to trim the tabletop flush with the aprons. Cut a top and two drop leaves from MDF (medium-density fiberboard) or solid-core veneer plywood. Sand the pieces, then paint or finish all four sides of each as desired.

Drill pilot holes and screw down through the new top into the old. Fill the holes with wood putty and touch up the finish.

Install drop leaf hinges (available at any woodworker's store) to support the leaves. Attach a caster to each leg, and you're ready to roll!

Cooking Centers

Do you or does someone in your family love to cook, or is cooking just a necessary task? Either way, having a well-planned cooking center makes meal preparation easier and more fun, or at least less of a hassle.

   Decisions about cooktop and wall ovens or ranges depend on your cooking style and the available space. No matter what appliances you choose, remember that cooking centers revolve around the cooktop. Landing space—the area to either side of the cooktop—should be at least 9" on one side and 15" on the other. If the microwave is part of the cooking center, allow an additional 15".

With the cooktop in one island and the sink in another there's plenty of room for two or more cooks in a relatively modest space. Although a raised shelf was placed behind the sink so it can't be seen from the adjoining room, the cooking center's countertop was left open to maximize its workspace.

In a kitchen where an island serves as landing space for the wall oven, there should be no more than 48" between the front edge of the counter and the front of the oven.

In addition to the efficient use of space, this kitchen is remarkable for its storage capacity and dramatic color scheme. The back side of the cooking center island is lined with open shelves that house a cookbook library. The armoire holds everything from Grandmother's china to a prized collection of pitchers. Even the window seat gets into the act with apothecary-style drawers on each end and storage drawers under the seat.

The cranberry painted walls and oak cabinets mirror the colors of the painted oak islands and limestone countertops. The armoire sports a distressed finish in colors that coordinate with the cabinetry without matching. This combinations strike a pleasing balance between deep and neutral colors. After all, too much of a good thing is...just too much.

It's one of those "chicken or the egg" questions. Appliances first? Or cabinets? In truth, those decisions need to be made at about the same time. You can't order cabinets without knowing the dimensions of the appliances, but you're not ready to finalize the appliances until you've selected the cabinets.

Why? Because you may want to order matching cabinet fronts for the refrigerator and dishwasher. And even if you don't, the finish on the cabinets should play a part in deciding the color of the appliances. For example, white appliances mixed with dark cabinets or black glass appliances set into light cabinets create color blocks within the room. That may not be a problem in large kitchens and may even be a good idea in very contemporary designs, but it could be distracting in smaller or more traditional-style kitchens. Stainless steel appliances are favorite choices, at least partly because their soft glow blends into almost every color scheme.

When it comes to appliances, color is more than a matter of taste. Oven windows with black mesh usually offer the clearest view; the white screens or grids in all-white models can make it harder to see what's cooking.

Picture perfect efficiency.

Although there's certainly room for others, this elegant kitchen is effi-
ciently arranged for one cook. Command central is directly in the center of the room:
The large cooktop, surrounded by plenty of prep space, stands opposite the sink, which
rests in the center of the island. The casual dining space on the far side of the island is easy
to reach when it comes time to serve everyday meals. During parties, that space is a perfect place for guests to lounge while preparations are under way—close enough for
conversation, but not underfoot.

*When the task lighting
doubles as accent lighting for
dining, make sure the
switches have dimmers. That
way, you can cook under
bright lights, dim the lights
for the meal, then return
them to full power while you
clean up.*

Cooking pasta for a crowd is a lot more convenient when you have a pot-filling faucet above the cooktop.

What a wonderful place to cook! The heat-resistant concrete countertops make ideal landing space for hot pans from the cooktop—or dishes from the nearby double ovens. The combination of concrete and subway tiles on the backsplash is simple but elegant, and oh-so-easy to clean up after cooking marathons. Splatters—even greasy ones—just wipe right off (as long as the grout lines are carefully sealed).

Vent hoods exhaust heat, moisture, grease, and cooking vapors from the air in your kitchen, protecting your cabinets and decorative surfaces—and your health. Normally, vents are installed with a ducting system that carries kitchen air to the outdoors. Local building codes may have specific ventilation requirements, so check with your building inspector or an HVAC contractor before buying a ventilation unit.

A true reflection of good taste, this cooking center features a stainless steel cooktop, gleaming metal vent hood and gorgeous metal tiles. Vent hoods are mounted above cooktops to catch rising heat, moisture, and grease. Vent hoods are either ducted or ductless. The ducted version uses a metal duct to vent air to the outdoors; a ductless vent simply recirculates air through filters. Ducted vent hoods are far more effective than ductless models. In fact, in many communities, ductless vents aren't allowed.

The National Kitchen and Bath Association recommends that every kitchen have a vent fan vented to the outside, and that the fan be capable of removing a minimum of 150 cubic feet of air per minute. Vent hoods are more important than you might think—one industry report indicates that inadequate ventilation can spread six quarts—*six quarts*—of grease throughout your home each year.

Vent hoods may be serious business, but they're also design opportunities.

Artistic panels make the vent hood the focal point of this kitchen. Any vent hood's primary reason for being is to provide ventilation, but here, as in many kitchens, it's also called upon to provide task lighting for the cooktop. The interior light fixtures are positioned to wash the backsplash, creating pleasant lighting for cooking.

The island and the large cabinets flanking the range are designed to create the impression of individual pieces of furniture.

In this compact kitchen, space is at a premium, but ventilation is still necessary. A vent hood/microwave unit provides both functions in one efficient, space-saving unit.

Going in an altogether different direction, the vent hood above this cooktop is concealed behind matching cabinet doors.

The downdraft system built into this stainless steel range makes a separate ventilation unit unnecessary, leaving space above the unit for cabinets.

Downdraft vents have blower units that vent through the back or bottom of a base cabinet. They are often used with modular ranges or cooktops, especially when they're installed in an island. Because a downdraft vent needs to work against the natural upward flow of heated air, it needs a more powerful motor than a standard vent hood.

Commercial-style cooktops are, by definition, rather large, and so are the vent hoods they require. Their sheer size offers design opportunities galore. These homeowners answered the challenge with a custom-built, tiled vent hood and backsplash combination.

Wow! When it comes to cooking units, the number of choices can make your head spin. Step into a home center or appliance store and you'll see a dizzying array of types, styles, sizes, and price ranges of products.

Choosing cooking units starts with deciding between gas and electric power. If you're working with existing space, it's usually far less expensive to use the same power source you currently have. If you're building or doing a major remodeling project, all options are open.

Remember that even gas units require a 120-volt, 20-amp outlet to provide power for the oven timers and flame-ignition modules.

If you like electric cooking, a smooth-top cooktop and a wall oven make an excellent combination. This island has loads of prep space on each side (the National Kitchen and Bath Association suggests at least 18" on one side) and storage all around. Here, the large center drawer holds plenty of pots and pans, and the smaller drawers are home to everything from spices to spatulas, hand towels to hot pads.

Smooth-top cooktops heat up in a flash, and they're easy to keep clean—fine characteristics for cooks-on-the-go. There is a price, though. Actually, there are several: Smooth tops typically are more expensive to purchase than coil burner cooktops, and they're more expensive to repair and replace. Plus, some models require flat-bottom cookware, which is another expense unless you already own it. Still, for many cooks, this popular combination is worth the expense.

Words to the Wise

The broad categories of cooking units are: range, cooktop, and wall oven. A *range* combines an oven and cooktop surface in one unit, a good choice when money or space is tight. A *cooktop* essentially is the burner portion of a range, with no oven. When you choose a cooktop, by default you'll also be choosing a separate oven or ovens.

• **Free-standing ranges** fit between cabinets or at the end of a row of cabinets.

• **Drop-in ranges** are unfinished on both sides and rest on a cabinet base.

• **Slide-in ranges** are unfinished on both sides and just slide into place between base cabinets.

• **Commercial-style ranges** are large, highly powered units that include four, six, or eight burners and an assortment of grills and griddles; they typically include several oven compartments as well. Burner output usually is 15,000 BTUs, much more than the 7,000 BTUs of standard burners. Commercial-style ranges are specially insulated, so they can be butted against walls or cabinets, and require heavy-duty vent hoods.

• **Commercial ranges** are generally not suited to home use, since they are not insulated well enough to meet code requirements and require complex, commercial-size ventilation units.

• **Drop-in cooktops** are installed in a hole cut in the countertop. Gas or electric, they include a variety of burners, some with interchangeable grills, griddles, and burners. Their controls are found on the top of the unit.

• **Commercial-style cooktops** overlap the cabinet case, so the controls are at the front of the unit. These cooktops include the same sort of variety of multiple burners, grills, and griddles as commercial-style ranges.

• **Single wall ovens** can be placed under drop-in cooktops or in full-height cabinets.

• **Double wall ovens** are placed in cabinets. Both single and double wall ovens are available in radiant, convection, microwave, or dual-duty products.

Plan a cooking center that fits your life.

When you're planning the kitchen, don't forget the microwave! It's so handy if you have children, and even gourmet cooks want a quick snack now and then. Although you can buy a microwave in every home center and discount store in North America, its selection and placement deserves the same careful thought as any other major appliance.

When built into the cabinets above a range, a microwave is positioned for adult use. That's fine if your family includes only adults, but not convenient if you have younger children who help with meal preparation or make their own snacks. (Standing on a chair to reach over the range or cooktop is not a good idea.)

Experts recommend that microwaves be placed so the bottom is 24 to 48" above the floor. However, 30 to 48" is the preferred range for average adult users, and 28 to 34" is typical for families that include children or smaller users.

Glass cabinet doors brighten a room, but clear glass lets everyone see exactly how organized you are. Obscured glass reflects light without giving away all your secrets.

An easy-to-clean range, built-in microwave, and plenty of prep space make this cooking center a joy to use. Landing space on either side of the range and refrigerator simplify meal preparation, especially when there's more than one cook in the kitchen.

If you have butcher block countertops, keep a cutting board handy. Cutting on the countertop could damage and stain it.

No detail was spared in planning this rustic kitchen. With an oversized gas range and a dramatic vent hood, the cooking center had an excellent foundation. A metal tile backsplash was added to preserve and protect the beautiful pine walls behind the range. The freestanding island is a convenient spot for food preparation, and the deep sinks handle large pots and pans with ease.

CHAPTER 4

Dining and Hospitality

When it comes to kitchen design, trends don't just come and go. They come and go, and come and go again. Eat-in kitchens have been in and out of fashion in several cycles since Colonial days, and kitchens have grown and shrunk correspondingly.

During the latest cycle, begun in the 1950s, eating and entertaining moved back into the kitchen, and kitchen designs expanded once again. In fact, virtually every home built in the last forty years provides at least some accommodations for eating in the kitchen; most homes built in the last ten years positively celebrate the idea.

If you're like most people today, you want to be able to eat and entertain in your kitchen. Once you've established that, the question becomes, "In what fashion?"

Is a harvest table too much? Peninsula or island space too little? Where will guests gather? These are questions that only you can answer, based on your family's style of living. As you look through the following pages, keep an eye out for designs and ideas that suit your family's patterns of cooking, eating, and entertaining.

A family who loves to entertain needs a kitchen that "works and plays well with others." In other words, a kitchen that meets the family's everyday needs, but is also arranged well for entertaining.

With its wide traffic aisles, this spacious kitchen is always ready for a party.

The island, framed by a raised dining surface, hosts both the cooktop and sink. Although the cook can talk with family members or guests while working, the raised counter nudges others to the opposite side of the island, conveniently out of the work triangle.

Favorite wines are stored in easy proximity to the bar area.

Barware sparkles from inside a lighted accent cabinet hanging directly above a bar-style sink.

Accent lighting, such as these pendants, is switched separately and
controlled with dimmers.

Double ovens offer plenty of capacity
when it's time to bake family favorites
or party delicacies.

What could be nicer than dinner in front of the fire on a cold winter evening? And with today's clean-burning, instant-on gas fireplaces, it's so easy and convenient.

In a kitchen with painted cabinets and a stained island, mixing a painted table and stained chairs is a nice touch.

In this Arts and Crafts inspired kitchen, a banquette nestles below a bank of windows. It's a lovely spot for meals, and with the table pulled
aside, comfortable seating for parties. Another advantage of a banquette: storage. Oodles
of easy-to-reach storage can be hidden beneath the seat cushions.

In not-so-big kitchens, ingenuity triumphs over limited square footage.

An extra-wide, cutting board—style pull out hides in the dark until meal time, then makes its entrance. A surface like this needs to be at least 24" long to accommodate a place setting, and 28 to 32" wide to serve two.

Drop leaves on each side of a peninsula rise to the occasion for din-
ners or parties, then fold away neatly. The cabinet opens to the front, leaving the sides free
for the space-saving drop-leaf mechanisms.

Color gives large presence to small spaces.

The contrast between this vivid blue wall and the white beadboard below sets the stage for a charming vintage-style dining area. The simple pendant light provides light without distracting your eyes from the framed prints and table settings.

Glass shelves produce the illusion that these black accessories are floating against the apple-green walls, making this corner look much bigger than it is. A sheet of glass balanced between a wall cleat and a stub wall serves dinner for one.

*Dollar*Wise

An heirloom butcher block like the one on page 98 is ideal, but you can build a countertop dining space even without an expensive antique. Start by building a countertop out of ³⁄₄" exterior-grade plywood, 4-mil. polyethylene sheeting, ¹⁄₂" cementboard, and hardwood edging or v-cap edge tile. Attach support blocking to the plywood with screws, and add unfinished furniture legs, which are available at home centers and woodworking stores.

Set tile with thin-set mortar and let it dry. Grout and polish the tile, and you've got your very own, custom-built, informal dining space.

One table. Many settings.

Finished to match
the cabinets, this
table appears to be built
in, but that's just an
illusion.

For everyday
meals, the table is
set perpendicular to
the wall of cabinets.

For parties, the table is shifted to the center of the room, an arrangement that makes it easier for guests to circulate.

*Idea*Wise

To emphasize the appearance of a peninsula extending from an island, change the flooring beneath it. For example, in a hardwood kitchen, set ceramic or stone tile in a shape to echo the peninsula, large enough for the surrounding seating.

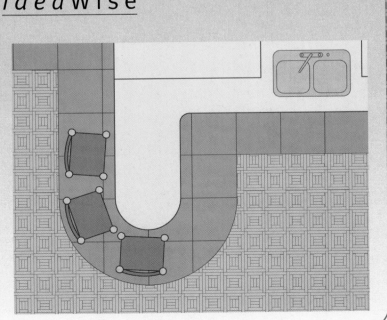

Although space was at a premium, the homeowner wanted an island that could double as eating space. She also wanted to use an heirloom butcher block that had once belonged to her grandmother.

By adding legs to the butcher block and attaching a custom-tiled countertop to one side, she created a unique and meaningful work and dining space for the family.

Furniture-quality legs and a center shelf support the butcher block beautifully.

Angled eating surfaces attached to the ends of the island take advantage of the available space in this long, narrow kitchen. The angles leave plenty of passage room around the island and add an interesting touch to the room.

*Design*Wise

Max Isley,
CKD, CBD, CMKBD

Hampton Kitchens
Wake Forest, NC

Plan dining and entertaining spaces to produce a comfortable flow for everyday dining as well as for parties. Think about where family members and guests will enter the kitchen and where they will stay once they're in the room.

• Create a snack or serving area within about 6 to 8' of the cooking area. Family members and guests will then be within comfortable distance of the cook without being underfoot.

• At a table or counter, provide at least 24" for each seated diner. If you wrap around the end of an island or table, allow a 36" return to comfortably accommodate two people at the corner.

• Think about clearance between seated diners and walls or furniture. A space of 24" is the minimum that allows you to avoid bumping the obstacle with the chair, but it takes at least 36" to be able to walk behind a seated guest.

• Don't automatically center a lighting fixture in an eating area. Decide what furniture you will use and where it will be, then position the lighting fixtures. Many times, it's best to set a fixture off center to leave room for furniture or artwork along the walls.

When the food preparation area and the dining area of a kitchen are open to one another but divided visually, neither should dominate.

A white brick wall anchors one side of this kitchen. To keep the food prep area from looking too heavy, the homeowners chose simple white cabinets, some with glass doors. Sunny yellow walls, framed by white cove molding, warm the whole room, and a glass-top table balances the whole equation.

The owners of this elegant kitchen wanted comfortable furnishings

that didn't compete with the stunning view. They established a delicate balance by selecting a glass tabletop subtly supported by stone pillars and chairs with cream upholstery that melds with the windows and trim. Then they added black-and-cream accents such as the floor covering and fabrics repeated throughout the room. Simple but stunning.

Repeated materials unify open-plan rooms.

This island is big enough for quick snacks and casual meals for two.

A sun-filled space nearby holds a table and chairs, ready to host more formal meals or larger groups.

Taupe tumbled stone shows up on the broad expanse of backsplash and then again in a border set into the island's countertop. The iron and oak of the barstools and dining chairs echo the appliances and the cabinetry, and their taupe and white upholstery complements the stone tile.

A glossy, raised surface, supported by steel corbels, rounds out the end of this
island and provides plenty of dining space for two without adding much to the footprint of the island.

CHAPTER 5

Lighting

Great kitchens have great lighting plans. Always. Take a look through this book, magazines, model homes, and the homes of your friends and family. Pretty soon, you'll see a pattern—the most attractive kitchens have excellent lighting. No matter how well equipped or how well laid out a kitchen is, it doesn't make the leap from good to great without efficient, attractive lighting.

Most people recognize that they need light in order to work comfortably in a kitchen. (Let's just say that no one wants to be using knives in the dark.) In response, many kitchens are built with most of the light concentrated in very bright central fixtures. But lighting the middle of the room and the ceiling isn't all that important. Getting light to the countertops, sink, and other prep and eating areas is.

The best way to light all those spaces is with individual sources. Recessed lights or track lights over a sink keep the area bright and shadowless even after the sun goes down. Pendants or spots over an island brighten valuable work and eating space. Strip lights on the underside of the cabinets reduce shadows. A pendant with a chrome-bottom bulb over the breakfast table provides soft light for the eating area.

You get the idea. The important thing is to come up with a plan that provides light for the many activities that take place in your kitchen and fits the style of the room. The photos throughout this chapter illustrate lots of ideas. Find your favorites and use them as starting points for creating a great lighting plan for your own kitchen.

If you're working with a kitchen designer, he or she is well prepared to make recommendations for lighting. If not, designers in home centers and salespeople at lighting stores are often very helpful. There are also professional lighting designers who, for a fee, will develop a lighting plan for you. You should have solid floor plans in hand before consulting with a lighting designer to take the best advantage of their expertise.

Words to the Wise

Ambient lighting sets the minimum level of lighting in a room, typically diffuse light from several sources. Windows, skylights, and overhead fixtures provide ambient light.

Task lighting provides brighter, functional light for individual work areas.

Accent lighting is subtle, indirect light that stresses points of decorative interest.

Recessed cans provide excellent general lighting. In insulated ceilings, make sure the cans are ventilated and the fixtures are rated for that purpose.

Under-cabinet lighting placed at the front edge of the cabinet reduces glare.

Lights concealed in cove moldings make ceilings look higher.

Light for dining areas should be controlled by dimmer switches.

In a well-lit kitchen, task, accent, and ambient light work together to create a comfortable environment for work and play.

Task lighting does just what its name implies—illuminates specific tasks. Task lighting should provide about three-fourths of the light in your kitchen.

Accent lighting emphasizes details, such as art or favorite collectibles. Like spices in cooking, accent lighting is added to taste.

Light colors and shiny surfaces require less lighting than dark, matte surfaces. Lighting a kitchen like this, with dramatic contrast between cabinet units, presents special challenges. This flexible, adaptable track lighting allowed the homeowners to use a variety of fixtures and to position them effectively.

To reduce glare from shiny surfaces, use frosted fixtures or bulbs rather than clear ones.

Don't be afraid to mix sizes and styles—even colors—of fixtures on one track. This track supports fixtures in two styles and several heights, delivering abundant light to individual task spaces.

When aimed at specific objects, track fixtures act as accent lights.

Keep the bottom of pendants about 36" above the surface of an island,
or about 30" above a dining counter or table—higher if the ceiling is higher. To avoid painful (and
potentially damaging) bumps in the night, hang the fixtures within the footprint of the island or counter.

Concealing lighting within display spaces gives favorite pieces the attention they deserve.
Tiny puck lights are an easy, inexpensive way to light display spaces.

Daylight is the primary source of ambient light for most kitchens during the day. As a general rule, the area of a kitchen's windows should equal at least 10 percent of its floor area.

A gorgeous bank of windows provides plenty of daylight in this charming kitchen. Their unique shape, the white trim, and the absence of window treatments all emphasize their brightness within the deep colors of the wallcovering.

Light from corner windows bounces off adjacent walls, further brightening any room.

Place lights high on walls, washing the walls with light, to make rooms feel more spacious.

*Dollar*Wise

To add light to the tops of cabinets without investing a lot of money, tape rope or twinkle lights just below the molding or trim. If the finish on the cabinets is dark, you might want to paint just the tops and back of the trim with gloss white paint to increase the reflection.

Skylights add wonderful, diffuse light. In this light-colored ceiling, light from the skylight is multiplied as it bounces off the rest of the ceiling and the walls. Skylights must be placed carefully. In hot climates, avoid south- or west-facing skylights or choose units that can be shaded in the afternoon.

Light from clerestory windows bounces off the ceiling and nearby walls, multiplying the ambient light they supply. In kitchens with high ceilings, placing windows above the cabinets doesn't sacrifice usable storage space and makes more sense than a standard soffit. And with uplights placed behind the framing for the upper cabinets, there's plenty of soft light from above, even when it's dark outside.

IdeaWise

Hide rope lights above a crown molding to create soft, comforting light to wash walls and ceilings. Install the crown molding 3 to 12" from the ceiling, using support blocks to hold it away from the wall. Cut a notch in the molding in an unobtrusive spot near a receptacle. Lay the rope lights in the trough between the wall and the molding. If you need more than one rope, remove the end caps and insert male/female connectors into the ends. Thread the cord down through the notch in the molding and plug it in. If you have the skills, you can hardwire low- or line-voltage rope lights into a nearby circuit.

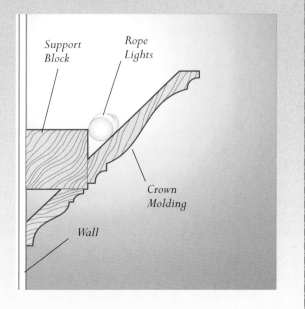

Support Block

Rope Lights

Crown Molding

Wall

The ceiling and beams are painted white to amplify and reflect light.

The beam supports track lighting for the island.

Each bank of windows is topped by track lighting, providing light in the evenings and on dreary days.

Under-cabinet fixtures light the countertop.

Window sashes separate the kitchen from the dining area without blocking light.

Glass doors let light pass through the cabinet uppers, highlighting the homeowners' collection of crystal.

Coordinating the lighting plan with the decorating scheme makes the most of both. This light, bright kitchen is the result of attention to details.

Contrast works miracles.
With white cabinets, appliances, and flooring, this kitchen could have looked cold and sterile. By using dark wallpaper and accessories, the homeowners provided contrast for the light to sparkle against. And look at that window in the backsplash area. Not large, but it's an eye catching feature that brings in just a little more light.

*Design*Wise

Connie Gustafson, CKD

Sawhill Custom Kitchens and Design, Inc.
Minneapolis, MN

Lighting is critical to the way your kitchen looks and to the way it works. Remember these suggestions:

• Place task light fixtures close enough to provide the proper amount of light for the tasks, and make sure the fixtures don't cast shadows on the work surface.

• Control ambient light with dimmer switches so you can adjust the light to create the effect you want.

• To add light inside cabinets with glass shelving and doors, use track or rope-type lighting at the front of the cabinet, along the sides. Add additional molding as necessary to hide the fixtures.

• If you use several pendants over an island, place them so each spread of light intersects with the light from the adjacent fixtures.

CHAPTER 6

Communication and Convenience

Folk wisdom is that the kitchen is the heart of a home. True, but in our busy world, it's also the nerve center, a place where communication, convenience, and comfort come together to serve and preserve a family's life.

Sometime during the 1970s and '80s, kitchen desks became almost standard equipment in new suburban homes. Despite their popularity, those desks weren't very practical—almost no one ever sat down at one for long, and the wasted space under them was a magnet for clutter. These days, kitchen desks have evolved into communications centers that include comfortable workspace, storage areas, message centers, and electronic equipment.

Electronics? Absolutely. In many kitchens, you'll find equipment that incorporates TV, music, and Internet access. Computers keep track of recipes, store grocery lists, and let you pay bills on-line. Some even have monitors that help you keep an eye on an infant napping in the nursery, teenagers hanging out in a basement recreation room, or visitors arriving at the front door.

All that equipment is great, but truly exceptional kitchens also make room for old-fashioned, face-to-face communication. A couple of cushy chairs. Maybe an ottoman or footstool. Good lighting. If you're really lucky, a fireplace.

In the next few pages, you'll see comfortable, attractive spaces where meals are created and served, work gets done, and people enjoy one another's company. Study them carefully for ideas you can incorporate into your own home.

Experienced kitchen designers report that most people considering a kitchen remodeling project want space that is, above all, versatile. Many potential remodelers dream of kitchens where they can supervise the kids' homework, pay bills, keep an eye on the evening news, and run a couple loads of laundry . . . all while dinner is cooking.

And, with careful planning, those dreams can become reality.

Set into a stunning wall of cabinets, this desk is flanked by bookshelves, file drawers, pigeonholes, and storage space. A true command center for the household.

The cherry trim coordinates with the desk surface, the door and drawer pulls, and the underlayer of the distressed finish.

A simple under-cabinet light illuminates the workspace.

Shelves hold a collection of cookbooks, reference manuals, and other family favorites.

Again, a desk space surrounded by **drawers,** cabinets, cubbyholes, and filing space pulls double duty in a kitchen. With the work surface cut at an angle, this desk takes maximum advantage of minimal space in this passageway to the kitchen.

Lights and glass doors transform otherwise wasted space into a dramatic display area.

Electrical receptacles and phone jacks are must haves for desk areas. Depending on your television preferences, Internet access, and computer systems, you may want to add cable jacks as well.

Framed by a cereal pantry and a cabinet filled with antique china, this window provides both light and an attractive view. In a clever use of space, the homeowners nestled a desk beneath the window and added a cookbook shelf below to discourage the clutter that sometimes collects under kitchen desks.

Elevating the food preparation area of this kitchen creates a sense of division without full walls. The long computer counter, flanked with drawers and filing cabinets, offers plenty of room to spread out books and papers for homework, household management, or Internet research and correspondence. Well-placed windows flood the area with light, making the small space feel spacious and open.

A well-designed corner nook shelters this home office. By angling the ceiling and adding a window, the homeowners created the sense of a distinct area within the room. Having a computer in the kitchen is surprisingly handy. It handles recipes, nutrition information, and grocery lists as well as the family finances and the children's homework.

Ingenuity wins again. With today's portable equipment and wireless Internet access, you can make efficient workspace even without the luxury of a permanent setup. A drop-leaf section on a cabinet base can be called into service or folded away, depending on the needs of the moment.

Some of us like it and some of us don't, but television is a daily fact of life for most families. Creating space for it just makes sense.

A large space like this calls for a large television. The cabinet case, which shields the back from view, is set at an angle so the screen can be viewed from the food preparation areas.

If you have a large kitchen and want to be able to see the television from several angles, set a cabinet case on a swivel.

A television doesn't have to take center stage. Set into a bank of cabinets, a small set isn't intrusive. And if you add doors that slide out from the sides and then fold closed, it can blend into the room when no one's watching.

Surrounding cabinets and cubbies give you places to store the remote and
DVDs or tapes. Installed in upper cabinets adjacent to an informal eating area, this small
TV is present without overwhelming the area.

Not every clever idea is complicated—sometimes you really can Keep It
Simple. This inexpensive portable stereo, controlled with a handheld remote, provides
music for the kitchen without taking up precious counter space.

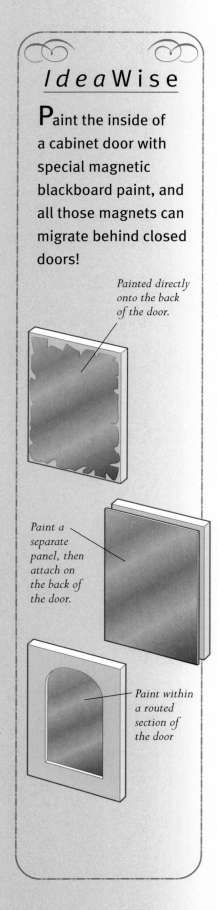

Sometimes communication can be as simple as a message board in a central location.

The wall in this dining area sports a large, framed blackboard where the family keeps lists, leaves messages for one another, and makes miscellaneous notes.

DollarWise

Large slate blackboards are heavy and can be expensive, but you can make an inexpensive substitute in just a couple of hours. Paint a piece of hardboard with blackboard paint, let it dry, then frame it with trim molding. Add some hanging hardware and you're ready for action.

A blackboard framed into the end of the cabinets acts as a message center in this compact kitchen.

Whether it's an adjacent family room or a small seating area, most homeowners find that the ultimate communication tool is room for the family to hang out in the kitchen and talk.

Not exactly a family room and far more than just a couple of chairs in the corner, a comfortable seating area brings this kitchen to life. It's a great place to lounge while meals are prepared and a wonderful place to wake up with coffee or unwind at the end of the day.

If you're lucky enough to have an area like this, furnish it with swivel chairs that can face the fireplace or the food preparation area, depending on the activity of the moment.

Kitchens that are open to adjacent rooms certainly encourage communication. This family room is set apart from the kitchen just a bit, but close enough for comfortable conversation. Another plus: the corner fireplace is clearly visible from both areas.

*Design*Wise

Stephanie J. Witt,
CKD, CBD, CMKBD

Kitchens by
Stephanie, Ltd.
Grand Rapids, MI

We find that most kitchen communications are brief, and the standard low desks are inefficient, awkward, and hard on the back. To avoid these issues:

• Raise the desk to 42" and incorporate a wide stack of drawers on both sides, including one or two lateral filing cabinet drawers.

• Place pigeonholes in the wall cabinets above the desk, and line the inside of the cabinet doors with cork. Install an electrical outlet and telephone line inside the cabinet to service a computer and portable phone.

• Enclose the area with tambour doors similar to those found on appliance garages. The doors may stay open most of the time, but everyone has days when they need to close doors over work in progress.

If you really want a seating area but don't think you have the room, look again with a more critical eye. You may have more options than you first realize.

When you adopt a less conventional attitude, even a chandelier in the middle of the room doesn't dictate that it be used as a dining area. You can remove the fixture and cover the electrical box with a blank plate painted to blend into the ceiling. Voilà! A seating area materializes before your eyes. With enough counter space and possibly a formal dining room, no one will ever miss another table.

The atrium area of this kitchen is furnished as a seating area rather than the more conventional dining space it might have been. The bank of windows and luxurious sofa are an irresistible combination the family appreciates every day.

Resource Guide

A listing of resources for information, designs, and products found in IdeaWise Kitchens.

Introduction

pages 4-5:   cabinets by
                    Plain & Fancy Custom Cabinetry
                    Oak Street & Route 501
                    Schaefferstown, PA 17088
                    1-800-447-9006
                    717-949-6571
                    www.plainfancycabinets.com

page 7:   kitchen design by
                    Kitchens by Krengel
                    1688 Grand Avenue
                    St. Paul, MN 55105
                    651-698-0844
                    www.kitchensbykrengel.com

pages 8 and 9:   kitchen design by
                    **Abruzzo Kitchens/
                    Jim Dase Kitchen Designer**
                    1105 Remington Road
                    Schaumburg, IL 60173
                    847-885-0500
                    www.abruzzokitchens.com

Walls, Floors and Ceilings

page 15:   kitchen design by
                    DeWitt Designer Kitchens
                    12417 Ventura Boulevard
                    Studio City, CA 91604
                    818-505-6901
                    www.dewittdesignerkitchens.com

page 16 (both photos):
                    cabinets and kitchen design by
                    Plain & Fancy Custom Cabinetry
                    Oak Street & Route 501
                    Schaefferstown, PA 17088
                    1-800-447-9006
                    717-949-6571
                    www.plainfancycabinets.com

page 17 (above): ceramic tile backsplash by
Crossville Porcelain Stone
P.O. Box 1168
Crossville, TN 38557
To find an authorized dealer
near you, call
931-484-2110
or go to
www.crossville-ceramics.com

page 17 (below): ceramic tile by
Meredith Tile
P.O. Box 8854
Canton, OH 44711
330-484-1656
www.meredithtile.com

page 18: concrete countertops by
Buddy Rhodes Studio, Inc.
2130 Oakdale Avenue
San Francisco, CA 94124
877-706-5303
www.buddyrhodes.com

page 19 (both photos):
cabinets by
Plato Woodwork, Inc.
Plato, MN 55370
1-800-328-5924
www.platowoodwork.com

page 21 (above): appliances by
Dacor
1440 Bridge Gate Drive
Diamond Bar, CA 91765
1-800-793-0093
www.dacor.com

page 21 (below): concrete countertops by
Buddy Rhodes Studio, Inc.
2130 Oakdale Avenue
San Francisco, CA 94124
877-706-5303
www.buddyrhodes.com

page 22: TimberGrass Flat Grain
Natural floor by
Teragren LLC
12715 Miller Road Northeast,
Suite 301
Bainbridge Island, WA 98110
206-842-9477
1-800-929-6333
teragren.com

page 24 (above): sheet vinyl floor by Armstrong
Flooring
page 25 (both photos):
hardwood floor by Armstrong
Flooring
Armstrong Flooring
Armstrong World Industries
2500 Columbia Avenue
Lancaster, PA 17603
717-397-0611
www.armstrong.com

page 26 (above): laminate flooring by
Wilsonart International, Inc.
2400 Wilson Place
P.O. Box 6110
Temple, TX 76503-6110
1-800-433-3222
www.wilsonart.com

page 26 (below): laminate flooring by
Pergo
Attention: Consumer Affairs
P.O. Box 1775
Horsham, PA 19044-6775
1-800-33-PERGO
(1-800-337-3746)
www.pergo.com

pages 27 and 28: kitchen design by
DeWitt Designer Kitchens
12417 Ventura Boulevard
Studio City, CA 91604
818-505-6901
www.dewittdesignerkitchens.com

page 29 (left): kitchen design by
Kitchens by Stephanie
3640 Thornapple Drive
Grand Rapids, MI 49546
616-942-9922
www.kitchensbystephanie.com

pages 30 and 31 (left):
cabinets by
Plato Woodwork, Inc.
Plato, MN 55370
1-800-328-5924
www.platowoodwork.com

Storage and Display

page 34: cabinets by
          Mill's Pride
          2 Easton Oval, Suite 310
          Columbus, OH 43219
          1-800-441-0337
          Mills Pride cabinets available
          exclusively at Home Depot
          stores

page 35: cabinets, furnishings and
          accessories by
          IKEA
          To shop, request a catalog, or
          find a store near you, call
          1-800-434-4532
          or go to
          www.IKEA.com

page 36 (above): cabinets by
          Mill's Pride
          2 Easton Oval, Suite 310
          Columbus, OH 43219
          1-800-441-0337
          Mills Pride cabinets available
          exclusively at Home Depot
          stores

page 36 (below): cabinets by
          KraftMaid Cabinetry, Inc.
          P.O. Box 1055
          Middlefield, OH 44062
          For more information or to
          locate an authorized dealer
          near you, call
          1-888-562-7744
          or go to
          www.kraftmaid.com

page 37: cabinets by
          Plato Woodwork, Inc.
          Plato, MN 55370
          1-800-328-5924
          www.platowoodwork.com

page 38 (below):   cabinet and drawer
                     accessories by
                     Poggenpohl U.S., Inc.
                     145 U.S. Highway 46 West,
                     Suite 200
                     Wayne, NJ 07470
                     www.poggenpohl.com

page 39 (above left and below left):
                     cabinet and drawer accessories
                     available through
                     Hafele America Co.
                     336-889-2322
                     www.hafeleonline

page 39 (above right and below right):
                     cabinets and accessories by
                     Plain & Fancy Custom Cabinetry
                     Oak Street & Route 501
                     Schaefferstown, PA 17088
                     1-800-447-9006
                     717-949-6571
                     www.plainfancycabinets.com

page 40 (above):   cabinets by
                     Plain & Fancy Custom Cabinetry
                     Oak Street & Route 501
                     Schaefferstown, PA 17088
                     1-800-447-9006
                     717-949-6571
                     www.plainfancycabinets.com

page 40 (below):   cabinets by
                     Plato Woodwork, Inc.
                     Plato, MN 55370
                     1-800-328-5924
                     www.platowoodwork.com

page 41:   cabinets by
                     Dura Supreme
                     300 Dura Drive
                     Howard Lake, MN 55349
                     1-888-711-3872
                     www.durasupreme.com

page 42:   cabinets by
                     KraftMaid Cabinetry, Inc.
                     P.O. Box 1055
                     Middlefield, OH 44062
                     For more information or to
                     locate an authorized dealer
                     near you, call
                     1-888-562-7744
                     or go to
                     www.kraftmaid.com

page 43:   cabinets by
                     Dura Supreme
                     300 Dura Drive
                     Howard Lake, MN 55349
                     1-888-711-3872
                     www.durasupreme.com

pages 44 and 45 (all):
                     kitchen design by
                     Kitchens by Krengel
                     1688 Grand Avenue
                     St. Paul, MN 55105
                     651-698-0844
                     www.kitchensbykrengel.com

page 46:   cabinets by
                     Plain & Fancy Custom Cabinetry
                     Oak Street & Route 501
                     Schaefferstown, PA 17088
                     1-800-447-9006
                     717-949-6571
                     www.plainfancycabinets.com

page 47 (both images):
                     kitchen design by
                     Kitchens by Krengel
                     1688 Grand Avenue
                     St. Paul, MN 55105
                     651-698-0844
                     www.kitchensbykrengel.com

pages 48 and 49 both images; page 50 (above):
                     cabinets by
                     Dura Supreme
                     300 Dura Drive
                     Howard Lake, MN 55349
                     1-888-711-3872
                     www.durasupreme.com

page 50 (below): cabinets by
KraftMaid Cabinetry, Inc.
P.O. Box 1055
Middlefield, OH 44062
For more information or to
locate an authorized dealer
near you, call
1-888-562-7744
or go to
www.kraftmaid.com

pages 51 and 52: countertops by
Cambria Corporation
636 Waverly St.
Palo Alto, CA 94301
650-328-9270
www.cambria.com

page 53 (both images):
kitchen design by
DeWitt Designer Kitchens
12417 Ventura Boulevard
Studio City, CA 91604
818-505-6901
www.dewittdesignerkitchens.com

page 54: kitchen design by
**Sawhill Custom Kitchens &
Design, Inc.**
@ International Market Square
275 Market Street, Suite 157
Minneapolis, MN 55405
 612-338-3991
www.sawhillkitchens.com

page 55: concrete countertops by
Buddy Rhodes Studio, Inc.
2130 Oakdale Avenue
San Francisco, CA 94124
877-706-5303
www.buddyrhodes.com

page 58: countertops by
DuPont Corian
offered by fine retailers
everywhere
For further information or to
find a retailer near you, call
1-800-4-CORIAN
(1-800-426-7426)
or go to
www.corian.com
To order samples, go to
www.coriansamples.com

page 59 (both images):
countertops by
Formica Corporation
Formica brand laminate offered
by fine retailers everywhere
For further information or to
find a retailer near you, call
1-800-FORMICA
(1-800-367-6422)
or go to
www.formica.com

Food Preparation and Clean Up

pages 62-63:   cabinets by
Plain & Fancy Custom Cabinetry
Oak Street & Route 501
Schaefferstown, PA 17088
1-800-447-9006
717-949-6571
www.plainfancycabinets.com

page 65:   cabinets by
KraftMaid Cabinetry, Inc.
P.O. Box 1055
Middlefield, OH 44062
For more information or to
locate an authorized dealer
near you, call
1-888-562-7744
or go to
www.kraftmaid.com

pages 66 and 67:   dishwashers by
Asko
AM Appliance Group
P.O. Box 851805
Richardson, TX 75085-1805
For more information or to
find a distributor near you, call
1-800-898-1879 or
972-238-0794
or go to
www.askousa.com

page 68:   cabinets by
Plato Woodwork, Inc.
Plato, MN 55370
1-800-328-5924
www.platowoodwork.com

page 71:   countertops by
Buddy Rhodes Studio, Inc.
2130 Oakdale Avenue
San Francisco, CA 94124
877-706-5303
www.buddyrhodes.com

page 72:   countertops by
Formica Corporation
Formica brand laminate offered
by fine retailers everywhere
For further information or to
find a retailer near you, call
1-800-FORMICA
(1-800-367-6422)
or go to
www.formica.com

page 73: sink by
Kohler
Kohler products available at
showrooms and retailers
worldwide
To locate a showroom or
retailer near you, call
1-800-4-KOHLER (456-4537)
or go to
www.us.kohler.com

pages 74-75: cabinets by
Plain & Fancy Custom Cabinetry
Oak Street & Route 501
Schaefferstown, PA 17088
1-800-447-9006
717-949-6571
www.plainfancycabinets.com

pages 76 and 77 (both images):
concrete countertops by
Buddy Rhodes Studio, Inc.
2130 Oakdale Avenue
San Francisco, CA 94124
877-706-5303
www.buddyrhodes.com

page 78: metal tile for backsplash by
Crossville Porcelain Stone
P.O. Box 1168
Crossville, TN 38557
To find an authorized dealer
near you, call
931-484-2110
or go to
www.crossville-ceramics.com

page 80 (above and below):
cabinets by
Plato Woodwork, Inc.
Plato, MN 55370
1-800-328-5924
www.platowoodwork.com

page 81 (above): appliances by
Amana
Amana is a brand in the family
of Maytag Appliances
Maytag Customer Service
403 West 4th Street North
Newton, IA 50208
For information or to locate a
retailer near you, call
1-800-843-0304
or go to
www.amana.com

page 81 (below): ceramic tile by
Daltile
7834 C.F. Hawn Freeway
Dallas, TX 75217
For more information or to
locate a dealer near you, call
214-398-1411
or go to
www.daltileproducts.com

page 82: kitchen design by
Kitchens by Stephanie, Ltd.
3640 Thornapple Drive
Grand Rapids, MI 49546
616-942-9922
www.kitchensbystephanie.com

page 84: appliances by
Amana
Amana is a brand in the family
of Maytag Appliances
Maytag Customer Service
403 West 4th Street North
Newton, IA 50208
For information or to locate a
retailer near you, call
1-800-843-0304
or go to
www.amana.com

page 85: cabinets by
Plato Woodwork, Inc.
Plato, MN 55370
1-800-328-5924
www.platowoodwork.com

Dining and Hospitality

pages 88-89:   kitchen design by
                Kitchens by Krengel
                1688 Grand Avenue
                St. Paul, MN 55105
                651-698-0844
                www.kitchensbykrengel.com

pages 90 and 92:   cabinets by
                Plato Woodwork, Inc.
                Plato, MN 55370
                1-800-328-5924
                www.platowoodwork.com

page 91:   windows by
                Andersen Windows, Inc.
                1-800-426-4261
                www.andersenwindows.com

page 93:   cabinets, furnishings, and
                accessories by
                IKEA
                To shop, request a catalog, or
                find a store near you, call
                1-800-434-4532
                or go to
                www.IKEA.com

page 98 (all images):
                kitchen design by
                Kitchens by Krengel
                1688 Grand Avenue
                St. Paul, MN 55105
                651-698-0844
                www.kitchensbykrengel.com

page 103:   island made of TimberGrass
                Flat Grain Natural panels from:
                Teragren LLC
                12715 Miller Road Northeast
                Suite 301
                Bainbridge Island, WA 98110
                For more information, call
                1-800-929-6333 or
                206-842-9477
                or go to
                teragren.com

Lighting

page 109:	lighting fixtures by **Tech Lighting** 7401 North Hamlin Skokie, IL 60076 For more information or to locate a showroom near you, call 847-410-4400 or go to www.techlighting.com
page 110:	concrete countertops by **Buddy Rhodes Studio, Inc.** 2130 Oakdale Avenue San Francisco, CA 94124 877-706-5303 www.buddyrhodes.com
page 111:	cabinets by **KraftMaid Cabinetry, Inc.** P.O. Box 1055 Middlefield, OH 44062 For more information or to locate an authorized dealer near you, call 1-888-562-7744 or go to www.kraftmaid.com
page 112:	windows by **Andersen Windows, Inc.** 1-800-426-4261 www.andersenwindows.com
page 113:	cabinets by **SieMatic** Two Greenwood Square 3331 Street Road Suite 450 Bensalem, PA 19020 For more information or to locate a dealer near you, call 1-888-316-2665 or go to www.siematic.com

Communication and Convenience

page 120: cabinets by
Plato Woodwork, Inc.
Plato, MN 55370
1-800-328-5924
www.platowoodwork.com

page 123 (below): cabinets, furnishings, and
accessories by
IKEA
To shop, request a catalog,
or find a store near you, call
1-800-434-4532
or go to
www.IKEA.com

page 125 (above): cabinets by
KraftMaid Cabinetry, Inc.
P.O. Box 1055
Middlefield, OH 44062
For more information or to
locate an authorized dealer
near you, call
1-888-562-7744
or go to
www.kraftmaid.com

pages 125 (below) and 126 (below):
kitchen design by
Kitchens by Krengel
1688 Grand Avenue
St. Paul, MN 55105
651-698-0844
www.kitchensbykrengel.com

Additional Resources

National Kitchen and Bath Association
For a free kitchen workbook, remodeling guide, and other helpful information, visit NKBA online at:

> www.nkba.org
> Or call 1-800-843-6522
> You can also write to:
> NKBA
> 687 Willow Grove Street
> Hackettstown, NJ 07840

For reviews, analysis and comparison of kitchen appliances and other consumer goods, go to:

> www.consumersearch.com
> www.goodhousekeeping.com

For buying guides, planning tools and additional how-to information, go to:

> www.homedepot.com
> www.lowes.com

For ideas, products, and advice on kitchen planning and design, go to:

> www.superkitchens.com

For ideas, products, advice on kitchen planning or to locate a kitchen professional near you, go to:

> www.kitchens.com

Photo Credits

front cover and title page: Getty Images.

back cover: (top left) Photo courtesy of Dewitt Designer Kitchens; (top right) Teragren LLC; (bottom left) ©Karen Melvin Photography; (bottom center) Photo courtesy of DuPont Corian; (bottom right) photo courtesy of Buddy Rhodes Studio, Inc./photo by davidduncunlivingston.com.

pp. 4-5: Photo courtesy of Plain and Fancy Custom Cabinetry.

p. 7: Photo courtesy of Kitchens by Krengel/ photo by Mims Photography, St. Paul, MN.

p. 8-9: Photos courtesy of Abruzzo Kitchens/Jim Dase Kitchen Designer.

p. 11: Photo courtesy of Plain and Fancy Custom Cabinetry.

p. 12: Getty Images.

p. 15: Photo courtesy of Dewitt Designer Kitchens.

p. 16: Photos courtesy of Plain and Fancy Custom Cabinetry.

p. 17: (top) Photo courtesy of Crossville, Inc.; (bottom) Photo courtesy of Meredith Collection.

p. 18: Buddy Rhodes Studio, Inc./photo by davidduncunlivingston.com.

p. 19: Photos courtesy of Koechel Peterson & Associates for Plato Woodwork, Inc.

p. 20: Beateworks, Inc. ©Andrea Rugg/ Beateworks.com

p. 21: (top) Photo courtesy of Dacor (www.dacor.com); (bottom) Photo courtesy of Meredith Collection.

p. 22: (left) Photo courtesy of Teragren LLC; (right) ©Dennis Krukowski.

pp. 24-25: (bottom left) ©Douglas Hill/ Beateworks.com; all other photos courtesy of Armstrong World Industries/Armstrong Flooring.

p.26: (top) Photo courtesy of Wilsonart International, Inc.; (bottom) Pergo.

p. 27-28: Photos courtesy of Dewitt Designer Kitchens .

p. 29: (left) ©David Leale for Kitchens by Stephanie, Ltd.; (right) ©Karen Melvin Photography for David Heide Design LLC, Minneapolis.

pp. 30-31: (left:) Photos courtesy of Koechel Peterson & Associates for Plato Woodwork, Inc.; p.31 (right) ©Micheal Arnaud/Beateworks.com.

p. 32: Beateworks, Inc./Tim Street-Porter/ Beateworks.com.

p. 34: Photo courtesy of Mill's Pride.

p. 35: Photo courtesy of IKEA Home Furnishings.

p. 36: Photo courtesy of Mill's Pride.

p. 37: Photo courtesy of Koechel Peterson & Associates for Plato Woodwork, Inc.

p. 38: (top) ©Andrea Rugg/Beateworks.com; (bottom) Photo courtesy of Poggenpohl U.S., Inc.

p. 39: (top & bottom Left) Photos courtesy of Hafele America, Co. (top & bottom right) Photos courtesy of Plain and Fancy Custom Cabinetry.

p. 40: (top) Photo courtesy of Plain and Fancy Custom Cabinetry; (bottom) Photo Courtesy of Koechel Peterson & Associates for Plato Woodwork, Inc.

pp. 41-42: Photos courtesy of Dura Supreme.

p. 43: Photo courtesy of Kraftmaid Cabinetry, Inc.

pp. 44-45: Photos courtesy of Kitchens by Krengel/photos by Mims Photography, St. Paul, MN.

p. 46: Photo courtesy of Plain and Fancy Custom Cabinetry.

p. 47: Photos courtesy of Kitchens by Krengel.

pp. 48-49: Photos courtesy of Dura Supreme.

p. 50: (top) Photo courtesy of Dura Supreme; (bottom) photo courtesy of Kraftmaid Cabinetry, Inc.

pp. 51-52: ©Karen Melvin Photography for Cambria Corporation.

p. 53: Photos courtesy of Dewitt Designer Kitchens.

p. 54: ©Saari & Forrai Photography for Sawhill Custom Kitchens & Design, Inc.

p. 55: Photo courtesy of Buddy Rhodes Studio, Inc.

p. 56: ©Karen Melvin Photography for Cornelius Interior Design, Minneapolis.

p. 57: ©Karen Melvin for Pappas Design, Minneapolis.

p. 58: Photo courtesy of DuPont Corian.

p. 59: Photos courtesy of Formica Corporation.

p. 60: Getty Images.

pp. 62-63: Photo courtesy of Plain and Fancy Custom Cabinetry.

p. 64: ©Roger Turk/Northlight Photography.

p. 65: Photo courtesy of Kraftmaid Cabinetry, Inc.

pp. 66-67: Photo courtesy of Asko-AM Appliance Group.

p. 68: Photo courtesy of Koechel Peterson & Associates for Plato Woodwork, Inc.

p. 69: ©Karen Melvin Photography for Corian.

p. 70: ©Karen Melvin Photography.

p. 71: Photo courtesy of Buddy Rhodes Studio, Inc.

p. 72: ©Karen Melvin Photography for Formica Corporation.

p. 73: Photo courtesy of Kohler Co.

pp. 74-75: Photo courtesy of Plain and Fancy Custom Cabinetry.

pp. 76-77: Photos courtesy of Buddy Rhodes Studio, Inc.

P. 78: Photo courtesy of Crossville Porcelain Stone.

P. 79: ©Jessie Walker

p. 80: Photo courtesy of Koechel Peterson & Associates for Plato Woodwork, Inc.

p. 81: (top) Photo courtesy of Amana; (bottom) Photo courtesy of Dal-Tile.

p. 82: ©Kaskel Architectural Photography, Inc. for Kitchens by Stephanie, Ltd.

p. 84: Photo courtesy of Amana.

p. 85: ©Pat Sudmeier for Koechel Peterson & Associates and Plato Woodwork, Inc.

p. 86: Getty Images.

pp. 88-89: Photo courtesy of Kitchens by Krengel.

p. 90: Photo courtesy of Koechel Peterson & Associates for Plato Woodwork, Inc.

p. 91: ©Karen Melvin Photography for Andersen Windows, Inc.

p. 92: Photo courtesy of Koechel Peterson & Associates for Plato Woodwork, Inc.

p. 93: Photo courtesy of IKEA.

p. 94: Karen Melvin Photography for Robert Gerloff Residential Architects, Minneapolis.

p. 95: Getty Images.

pp. 96-97: (all) ©Karen Melvin Photography for Woodshop on Avon, Minneapolis.

p. 98: (all) Photos contributed by Kitchens by Krengel/photo by Mims Photography, St. Paul, MN.

p. 99: ©Karen Melvin Photography for YA Architecture, Minneapolis.

p. 100: ©Jessie Walker.

p. 101: ©Karen Melvin Photography for Armstrong World Industries.

p. 102: ©Karen Melvin Photography.

p. 103: Photo courtesy of Teragren, LLC.

p. 104: Photo Courtesy of Mill's Pride.

p. 106-107: ©Karen Melvin Photography.

p. 108: ©Jessie Walker.

p. 109: Photo courtesy of Tech Lighting/ photo by Les Boschke; designer: Gregory Kay; location: Kay residence, Chicago, IL.

p. 110: Photo courtesy of Buddy Rhodes Studio, Inc./photo by davidduncunlivingston. com.

p. 111: Photo courtesy of Kraftmaid Cabinetry, Inc.

p. 112: ©Karen Melvin Photography for Andersen Windows, Inc.

p. 113: Photo courtesy of SieMatic Corporation.

p. 114: ©Jessie Walker.

pp. 115-117: ©Karen Melvin Photography.

p. 118: Getty Images.

p. 120: Photo courtesy of Koechel Peterson & Associates for Plato Woodwork, Inc.

p. 121: ©Karen Melvin Photography for Arteriors Architecture.

p. 122: (top) ©Karen Melvin Photography Locus Architecture, Minneapolis; (bottom) ©Jessie Walker.

p. 123: (top) ©Karen Melvin Photography McNulty Homes and Gigi Olive Interior Design; (bottom) Photo courtesy of Ikea Home Furnishings.

p. 124: (both) ©Karen Melvin Photography for (top) Audio Video Interiors Magazine; (bottom) YA Architecture, Minneapolis.

p. 125: (top) Photo courtesy of Kraftmaid Cabinetry, Inc.; (bottom) Photo contributed by Kitchens by Krengel; photo by Mims Photography, St. Paul, MN.

p. 126: (top) ©Karen Melvin Photography for McMonigal Architects, LLC., Minneapolis; (bottom) Photo contributed by Kitchens by Krengel/photo by Mims Photography, St. Paul, MN.

p. 127: ©Karen Melvin Photography for Keith Waters and Associates, Minnetonka, MN.

p. 128: ©Karen Melvin Photography for McNulty Homes, Minneapolis, MN.

p. 129: ©Karen Melvin Photography for Paragon Designers and Builders, Minnetonka, MN.

p. 130: (top) Photo courtesy of Plain and Fancy Custom Cabinetry; (bottom) Getty Images.

p. 132: ©Tim Street-Porter/Beateworks.com.

p. 135: Getty Images.

p. 137: Getty Images.

Index

Also from

CREATIVE PUBLISHING INTERNATIONAL

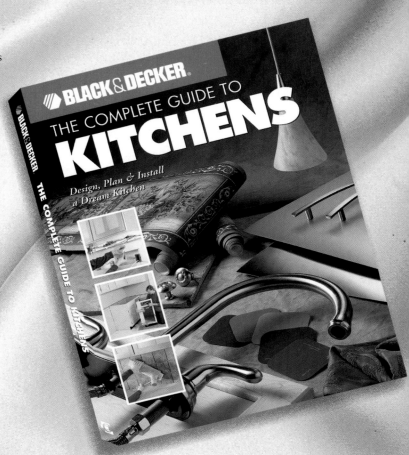

The Complete Guide to Kitchens

*W*hether it's a cosmetic facelift or a tear-it-out-and-start-over project, this book contains everything you need to plan and create the kitchen of your dreams.

ISBN 1-58923-138-4

CREATIVE PUBLISHING INTERNATIONAL

18705 LAKE DRIVE EAST
CHANHASSEN, MN 55317

WWW.CREATIVEPUB.COM